BULL & BUSH

My music business adventures
with Kate Bush, Queen,
Paul McCartney, The Sex Pistols,
Pink Floyd, Cliff Richard,
The Stones and more

BRIAN SOUTHALL

To Bernard
Enjoy the memories
best

pop publishing

Brian S

BULL & BUSH
Brian Southall
First published 2023 by Poppublishing

Published in paperback and ebook

For further information about this book please contact
poppublishing@gmail.com

Cover design: David Roberts
Cover photos: Michael Putland, Evening Standard, Daily Mirror, John Minihan, EMI

For Alyssa

It's my past
but the future is hers xx

ACKNOWLEDGEMENTS

As always the author's thanks go to David Roberts at Poppublishing for his support, valuable assistance and technical knowhow. Also, thanks go to all the people I worked with, those who crossed my path - and maybe crossed swords with me - during my time in the 'music biz'. It was fun and I hope they all enjoyed it as much as I did.

INTRODUCTION

I should firstly explain that last year (2022) I wrote and published a memoir entitled *A Saucerful of Tea*. It was, like so many things, a lockdown project, which covered a decade in my life from teenager to twenty something when I earned a crust as a journalist.

It went from my time as a cub reporter to sports editor (the youngest and, it has to be said, cheapest in the country) on local papers before four years on best-selling music publications such as *Melody Maker* and *Disc*, before I moved into the record business working for some of the best known and biggest music companies in the world.

Some of you may have bought that first effort (my thanks) while it passed others by. Now, here is the follow-up, covering those years from the seventies through to the 2000s when I worked with some of the most successful, notorious and famous artists.

Having swapped interviewing pop stars to actually working with them, I am able to tell tales about the Carpenters, Rolling Stones, Beatles (together and apart) Pink Floyd, Cliff Richard, Kate Bush, Queen, Sex Pistols, Phil Collins and the Corrs alongside some stories (and a few secrets) which show how the record industry worked back then.

Over the years, since my debut as an 'author' in 1982, I have been fortunate to have had more than 20 books published, covering the music business and major artists. Some of these titles were easy to write, some were simply labours of love, while a few required me to jump through some hoops in order to get the job done. Now you can, as newspaper sellers used to say, "read all about it."

Bull & Bush (a lot of one and some of the other - you decide) will, I hope, trigger some memories, offer some insights into a long-established, much loved and occasionally troubled business and - most of all - entertain you.

Brian Southall 2023

Chapter 1

IF I WERE A CARPENTER

It's really up to you. I don't mind whether you do it in the voice of Bamber or Jeremy, but this is your starter for 10: What connects an album topping trumpeter of East European heritage, a Kentucky Derby winning owner and an American septuagenarian comedy icon?

The answer, of course, is A&M Records, where the 'A' is trumpeter Herb Alpert, the 'M' is horse-owning promo man Jerry Moss and the funny man is Groucho Marx who released a live double album for the label in 1972.

I learnt this little nugget of music business trivia when I left being a music journalist to become a record company press officer in the late summer of 1973. My *Disc* colleague, Mike Ledgerwood, had gone to A&M before me and then hired me as his assistant where we both employed the principle that had been adopted by all rock writers turned PRs: we might not know what to do, but we did know what *not* to do that would piss off journalists.

Over-hype, ludicrous claims about an artist's credibility, comparisons with the great and good that had gone before and ambitious predictions about a record's chart potential were all the things we tried to avoid as we persuaded writers to interview our acts or review their records out of the hundreds released each week back then.

Having joined the label, which was founded in Los Angeles 1962, I was then treated to the second episode in the Groucho Marx meets A&M story. When he was told that the record company wanted to release a live album of his Carnegie Hall show, Marx apparently looked bemused and asked who they were. Either a company executive, his lawyer or the producer informed him that A&M was owned by Herb Alpert, who was the 'A', and Jerry Moss, who was the 'M'. Marx was still not convinced and whoever was doing the explaining then told him, or so the story goes, "You know Herb Alpert... Herb Alpert and the Tijuana Brass; you know them." Groucho's classic reply was, "Well, not all of them." It was a story that was part of A&M's history, alongside the fact that they bought and moved into Charlie Chaplin's old film studio in Hollywood and made it their offices in 1966.

In London we occupied a couple of floors above the Steinway Pianos showroom in George Street in the fancy Mayfair district. Those premises came complete with a grand staircase that led up to our offices where Managing Director Derek Green, A&R chief Dave Margerison, promotion head Tony Burfield and designer Mike Doud (plus the press office) all did their business. The roster of acts included The Carpenters, Billy Preston, Paul Williams, Bill Withers, Stealers Wheel, Gallagher & Lyle, The Strawbs, Rick Wakeman and an emerging new group called Supertramp.

Green, I was told, was a card-carrying member of the Labour Party who drove a Rolls Royce. And while he never tried to politically recruit me, nor did I ever get to ride in his fancy car, I did recognise that he was quite young for such a prestigious position; I later found out that he was in fact just 28 - and only two years older than me.

Doud, the American head of the label's in-house art department, eventually returned to his homeland and went on to great fame if not fortune by winning the 1979 Grammy for Best Album Package for his work on Supertramp's *Breakfast In America* cover. He is also recognised as the co-designer of Led Zeppelin's 1975 album *Physical Graffiti*.

In the late sixties and early seventies, A&M wasn't the most successful record label around as they fought against the established majors such as EMI, Decca, Pye, Philips, CBS and RCA. In fact between July 1968 – when founder Herb Alpert entered the UK Top 20 with 'This Guy's In Love With You' – and the time I joined, five years later, they had amassed a total of just ten Top 20 hits. The Carpenters led the way with three, followed by two from the Strawbs and one each from Carole King, Waldos de Los Rios, Stealers Wheel and Hudson Ford. The only number one album was The Carpenters *The Singles 1969-73*. Things were a little different in America where Alpert and The Carpenters were still the main hit makers until founder Moss, realising that his label had no acts on the bill at the influential 1967 Monterey Pop Festival, set about upgrading the roster with the likes of Joe Cocker, Cat Stevens, Billy Preston and Free.

One of these acts was involved when I began my new career playing a small part in a five-star, star-studded production involving the only non-Beatle musician to be credited on a record by the fab four, alongside arguably Britain's longest surviving rock band. My task was to go to Vienna to join Billy Preston who was on tour with (and acting as the keyboard player for) the Rolling Stones. The Stones' European tour opened in Austria's capital city on September 1st, 1973, and I was joined there by Ledgerwood and an assortment of company execs from America. They had all flown in to support Preston, who had hit No.2 in the Billboard US single chart with 'Outa Space' a year earlier, although Europe was apparently not as excited as the record peaked at 44 in the UK. But perhaps, like the rest of us, they were more excited about seeing the Stones in action.

Preston and the Stones were all staying in some fancy chateau outside Vienna and that was where we all assembled on the day of the show. There was little or no interest from the press in Preston (which made me redundant). They were all focussed on the Stones – and Mick Jagger and his wife Bianca in particular. The pair were being chaperoned by PR guru Les Perrin alongside the WEA UK press team of Annie Ivil and Moira Bellas who, in my previous existence as a journalist, had arranged my interviews with the likes of Randy Newman, the magnificently named all-girl group Fanny and Bread's David Gates.

Having chatted with Preston, who was not at all bothered about the media's disinterest in him and his God Squad band, I had the joy of taking tea and Austrian cakes with Charlie Watts and Bill Wyman who, bizarrely, were also of no interest to the press and they were equally happy with the situation. Enjoying afternoon tea as the news hounds clamoured to get a word from, or even better, a photo of the band's leader and his missus, seemed like an odd moment of sanity in the heady world of sex, drugs and rock'n'roll.

There was an after show party in a posh Vienna restaurant where Jagger skipped off early after doing a brief meet and greet round the tables but, surprise, surprise, he didn't recognise me from our earlier meeting backstage at Southend Odeon in 1965. Meanwhile, bandmate Richards and Preston slipped under the table in the hope that their antics (legal or otherwise) would go unnoticed. Before the night was out, Richards had very loudly offered anybody and everybody a lift with him in his Ferrari when the band travelled on to Germany for their next show. But nobody was brave/foolish enough to take him up on what would have been a fab tale to tell the grandchildren – assuming you survived.

As Preston and the Stones made their way to Mannheim, I travelled back to London relieved that I had avoided a possible confrontation with German border guards as they eyed me up as a passenger in Keith Richards' car. But bizarrely Heathrow Airport and Britain's customs officers proved to be no less vigilant when it came to the Rolling Stones and those associated with them.

I came back with a load of invitations for the people at A&M to a special Rolling Stones party being held during their three UK shows the following week. Called over for a chat and luggage search – presumably because my long hair, beard and gaudy but up to date gear made me look like a second rate musician – the powers that be found the invites ... and the words "Rolling Stones party."

This set all sorts of alarm bells ringing and brought out the rubber gloves and the sniffer dog as I was subjected to a full body search which, much to the disappointment of the 'uniforms', revealed nothing untoward. And to add insult to injury I never made it to the show or the party

If not quite a party, I was on duty at the Rainbow Theatre in London on December 13 and 14 when Lou Reizner, who had linked his Ode record label with A&M, put on two performances of The Who's rock opera *Tommy* for charity. It was not recorded for release but Green and the UK company gave support to the event which meant we got free tickets. I went along with my wife Pat and her friend to see Roger Daltrey, David Essex, Roy Wood, Marsha Hunt, Roger Chapman, Jon Pertwee and Viv Stanshall perform Peter Townshend's story of the "deaf dumb and blind kid who sure plays a mean pinball." Janet, who worked with Pat, was a devoted fan of Essex and I surprised her by taking her backstage in the interval to say hello to her hero. But there was a problem. A very drunk Stanshall (no surprise there) was collapsed on the floor behind the dressing room door making it difficult to get in. However, once he had been unceremoniously shoved aside, Janet got her meet and greet moment and the bonus of a chat with Roger Daltrey until The Who's lead singer announced his departure, explaining that he had to "go and splash me boots."

A month or so later I was on duty again but this time at the Royal Festival Hall where Rick Wakeman performed his work *Journey To The Centre of The Earth*. Featuring actor David Hemmings as the narrator, the show was recorded live and set to become the label's second UK number one album in May 1974. Wakeman, who almost went broke funding the project, wanted to celebrate the event with a party and was keen to have one of his heroes give a private performance. But the best laid plans to get Tommy Cooper to come along after he had finished a show somewhere in London's West End fell foul of A&M's money men when the comedian asked for a cash payment of many thousands of pounds for a 30-minute cameo. And it was obvious that Wakeman didn't have the cash. No money no Tommy!

Having successfully survived the Preston/Stones experience, two *Tommy* shows and Wakeman's night out, and with the UK entering a three day working week introduced by Conservative Prime Minister Edward Heath in January 1974, I moved on when the most popular

American brother and sister singing act prepared to tour Britain.

After a week of dates in Europe – which my boss Ledgerwood had put himself down for - The Carpenters arrived in Britain in February and I was on the road for the first time as a press officer for a working, much in demand, multi-million selling act, whose shows went on despite parts of the country being without heating and lighting for long periods until early March.

Looking back, it seems odd that music tours still went on with hotels and clubs open for business too but Richard and Karen began their tour in Glasgow on February 18 and I flew to Scotland to join the party. After Glasgow, it was on to Manchester in a private jet and that was where my problems began as I took some pills (prescribed of course) and champagne which left me the worse for wear and certainly unable to host the duo's press conference. I can't remember who came off the bench to replace me but I took to my bed to try and sleep it all off only to be disturbed by a phone call from the hotel receptionist. She was insisting that two men at the front desk were there to see me. I hung up but she called back and in slightly hushed tones told me who they were. "It's a Mr Law and a Mr Summerbee" she said and when I asked her to repeat herself, she explained, "Denis Law and Mike Summerbee."

"Send them up" was my instant reply and they duly arrived at my hotel room door – two of the most famous footballers in the land. It turned out they wanted tickets to the Carpenters show that night and had been told to find me at the hotel and I would sort out the tickets. And that I did, but only after an impromptu game of footie in the hotel corridor with me in goal, Summerbee crossing a cushion and Law jack-knifing to head home.

We met up again after the show, and went to the Slack Alice nightclub owned by football idol George Best. I sat with Karen Carpenter who was fascinated by the long-haired young man who was surrounded by a host of mini-skirted girls who hung on his every word. When she asked who he was, I said "That's George Best" which was when she replied, "Who's he?" At that point Miss Carpenter and I ceased to be best buddies!

The Carpenters' tour went on through Liverpool, Southport, Bristol, London and finally Birmingham on February 27 and as a first close-up foray into the world of touring it was an eye-opener. The daughter of the band's manager Sherwin Bash was going out with (and sharing a room with) Richard Carpenter which was fine until we found out her name was Randy Bash and then all bets were off as we dubbed her Randy Bang and giggled a lot.

Mrs Bash was also on the tour with I think the Carpenters' mum and another lady and they – with Karen – held regular needle point sessions backstage which was as raucous as it got in the green room. Meanwhile, Mr Bash was on patrol nightly to make sure we all attended every show on the tour – and it was two shows a night every night - which, for someone not in love with the Carpenters music, was a tough way to earn a living. In truth I, and my A&M colleagues on the tour, worked out some rotas and excuses so we could each have a night off. Typical excuses included a dodgy takeaway or the early signs of a sore throat ... we were only thinking of the band's well-being and didn't want to pass anything on!

There was also a strict no drugs policy for the band – and presumably for us in the backroom as well although nobody ever said so – and that meant that whenever there was a scare about being caught with marijuana (and that's all there was), we became drug mules. It seemed that the main culprit was the lovely and hugely talented guitarist Tony Peluso, the man behind the epic guitar solo on 'Goodbye To Love', and his stash was stored in a weighty plastic bag which we took ownership of on more than one occasion with certain people taking a dip in the bag as a carriage charge.

None of it was very rock'n'roll although the stay in Bristol brought some fun to the proceedings as comedian Larry Grayson was staying at the same hotel. He was in his finest camp mode in the bar where, as we took a night cap (sans any Carpenters or Bash's), he attempted to get to grips with a young waiter while one of the guys from the tour's promoters searched for the prostitute he'd booked. Little did he know that she, having been made an offer she couldn't refuse, had gone off with one of the band who in order to turn the lady's head had borrowed the £15 fee from me. In a state of desperation the band member had come to me, explaining that he had no English money and he was certain that his Yankee dollars would cut no ice with a good West Country girl who knew her business. I don't know what he got for his money but I do know I never saw it again, although I did claim it back as a legitimate PR expense.

Neither Richard nor Karen did any actual one-on-one interviews with the press but attended press conferences along the way – which I oversaw in a most professional manner after the Manchester incident – and regularly did meet and greets with the winners of local newspaper and radio competitions. There were also lots of signed photos to hand out at the stage doors and it fell to me and one of my colleagues to autograph loads of glossy black and white 10x8 pictures for these devoted fans. I think I was Karen but who knows. If it was good enough for The Beatles it was good enough for Dick & Ren.

The photo to my wife Pat that Richard and Karen DID sign

Near the end of the tour, the Carpenters did a special one-off show at London's *Talk of The Town* club in aid of a charity – might have been the Royal Variety Club – and it was there that Karen gave the band a major talking-to. She was a perfectionist in all she did and maybe that's why she seemed to me a little less than happy. In fact throughout the tour she kept to herself and was never a great conversationalist, joke teller or one for small talk. The saddest part was that she didn't seem to enjoy being a hugely talented and highly successful musician. During rehearsals at the *Talk of The Town*, she turned on the band when they joked around and deliberately messed up a couple of intros. It was then that

Bash stepped in and told her to calm down and cut the guys – after a month on the road and now doing a 'freebie' – a bit of slack. Thankfully, as the musos grumbled, she took his gentle chiding on board and the band played on.

After the tour, there was something of a surprise to come for all of us at A&M who were involved (and some who weren't but were still important) as we each received a letter from Sherwin Bash – posted within days of him returning to his Beverly Hills office – thanking us on behalf of himself and Karen and Richard for "being fantastic." And it came with a prezzie. In a leather jewellery box, together with a note personally signed by Richard and Karen, was a ring which had words cut out of the gold which spelled on one side 'love' and on the other 'fuck'.

Who'd have thought it - a rude ring from The Carpenters!

Of all the gifts in all the world, this wasn't the one you expected to get from the Carpenters. Maybe I had misjudged them after all.

Sometime in March 1974, Derek Green announced his plans to relocate A&M from the swanky Mayfair offices to somewhere maybe hipper, perhaps more credible and certainly less expensive. The plan was to move to Parsons Green in West London but it made me consider my future with the company. Getting from my home in Chelmsford to Liverpool Street and then across to Oxford Circus had been more than do-able (especially as nobody in the record business started work before 10am) but travelling on the Circle Line for 14 stops and then changing to the District Line to a station just one stop from Putney Bridge was something else. I did my calculations and worked out that it meant at least an hour on the underground with no buffet car or toilet. So outrageous was the prospect that I resigned – but only after I had lined up a new job. As A&M didn't make any hugely lucrative offer to make me stay, I left to join the company dubbed "The Sound of Young America".

Chapter 2

SOUL TRAIN

"The Sound of Young America" referred to Motown, when the company emerged in the early sixties, although when I got there it was known as Tamla Motown which was the name Motown adopted internationally to cover records released outside the US. In Britain the giant EMI company had a licensing agreement with Motown to release records by the likes of The Supremes, Marvin Gaye, and The Miracles which were originally destined to appear on Stateside, a label created by EMI for repertoire it licensed from American labels such as Motown, ABC, United Artists and Vee Jay.

It was in June 1964 when the first Motown acts debuted in the UK chart - albeit on Stateside - thanks to Mary Wells' 'My Guy' which was followed by The Supremes giving the label its first No.1 single with 'Baby Love' in November of the same year.

While on *Disc* I had written about Tamla Motown's artists and worked closely with the label's press officer Phil Symes. So, when Phil told me he was leaving I seized the opportunity to join EMI. I have no recollection of any interview but on April 1 1974 – yes it was April Fool's Day

- I became head of press for Tamla Motown and found myself based in the company's famous Manchester Square offices. Those offices featured on the cover of The Beatles first album *Please Please Me*, where the band are leaning over a rail on the first floor as photographer Angus McBean snapped them from the ground floor lobby.

Among my colleagues was Paul Prenter, the head of radio and TV promotion who later left to befriend Queen's Freddie Mercury and was portrayed truthfully in the film *Bohemian Rhapsody* as something of a devious and untrustworthy hanger-on. There was also Gordon Frewin who was in charge of organising release schedules and production and could have chosen Tamla Motown album catalogue numbers as his specialist *Mastermind* subject and he would have got every question right ... all of the STML, STMA and TMSP prefixes.

A month before I joined Tamla, Stevie Wonder had toured the UK but sadly I missed that show and he was among a long list of major Motown acts who didn't visit the UK during my time as their press representative in Britain. There was also Diana Ross, Marvin Gaye, Smokey Robinson, The Temptations and The Jackson 5 who did actually plan a British tour for June 1974 but cancelled it over security concerns. However, Junior Walker and Edwin Starr toured together, while Syretta came over to plug her album *Your Kiss Is Sweet* which involved a bunch of interviews but mostly because she was married to Stevie Wonder.

The Walker/Starr tour included a show in Manchester and it was this that brought home to me the difference between A&M's attitude to PR and EMI's which was best described as cheapskate. I took four journalists to the show in a gold, (shit-coloured) company Morris Marina – five of us in a saloon car for over 200 miles each way – and brought them back the same night as an overnight stay would have caused some hair pulling and foot stamping in accounts. I recall that we did stop at a motorway service station on the way back for a toilet break (which was free) and the limited amount of refreshments I thought I could swing on my expenses. Edwin Starr agreed to give a few interviews in the flat he rented in Kensington and among the journalists I invited there was a pretty young lady from a national tabloid. Starr was dressed for the part in a rather lurid dressing gown which, with the girl sitting opposite him and me just to her side, he let drift open to reveal that he was not wearing any underpants. Could have been an accident, I don't know but it was not a pretty sight and, while I made my excuses and left, the lady (seemingly unfazed) apparently stuck to the task in hand as the interview duly appeared a week later.

As an American licensed label (and perhaps a poor relation) within EMI - alongside the likes of MCA and Elektra/Asylum – we got moved around a bit and at one time had offices above the NatWest bank in Baker Street on the opposite corner to where The Beatles had their famous Apple boutique. My old friend Philip Lynott, from Thin Lizzy, popped in a couple of times for lunch – and to flirt with as many ladies as possible while adding to his collection of Tamla albums – but one of the more surprising visitors were a band that EMI had signed a couple of years earlier and who had notched up their first UK hits a month before I joined. EMI's legendary promotion man Eric ("monster, monster") Hall brought all four members of Queen round to our tiny two office headquarters of Tamla Motown where they set about cleaning out my album cupboard. And even off duty, they turned up in their finest rock'n'roll outfits with much satin, silk and fur which was obviously the everyday outfits they wore to the shops. This was my first encounter with Freddie, Brian, Roger and John but they would figure large later in my life with the stars.

During my Tamla time, an enthusiastic and diligent young Conservative had written to the label c/o of EMI, 20 Manchester Square, London W1, asking for a Tamla Motown person to attend a Young Conservatives meeting and give the members a talk. Needless to say he got no reply. As a result, he wrote to Berry Gordy, founder of the Motown empire, in Detroit complaining about EMI's response (or lack of) to his request. As a consequence my boss, Bob Mercer, duly ordered me to go off and talk to the Young Conservatives of Bexley in Kent. The only two things I remember about the evening were that the former Prime Minister, Edward Heath, sat silently at the back of the room – he had been elected MP for Bexley back in 1950 – and the audience was more interested in pop star gossip than the history and workings of Motown. Having made my debut as a public speaker, I then realised there was a circuit out there which involved all sorts of societies passing on info about anyone they could get as a freebie.

Over the years I ended up speaking at a host of Young Conservative meetings (I never made it to a Labour or Liberal event), including one where I was refused entry for not wearing a tie. Fortunately, some old buffer found me a splendid Conservative club tie which went well with my hip and happening ensemble. I also gave talks to Young Farmers, college students, sixth formers and even a gathering of prisoners.

After the prison talk, one inmate was so moved that he insisted on writing long letters to me asking about his chances of getting a recording contract or one of our acts recording one of his songs. I was able to convince him that as Motown was an American company we didn't sign UK acts and he should contact the EMI A&R (artists & repertoire) department instead. Two thoughts – we did sign a London-based band called Slowbone to the subsidiary Motown label Rare Earth but I never told him this - so did he come out of nick to forge a career as a best-selling singer or songwriter ... or both?

In June 1975, Motown in the US decided to take their UK subsidiary away from EMI and go independent with their own sales, marketing, promotion and press people. Bizarrely it didn't happen and the company's licensing deal with EMI was renewed within months but not before I had been let go. The man destined to be in charge of the newly independent Tamla Motown operation, John Marshall, was not my biggest fan (nor me his it has to be said) and he made it quite clear that I did not figure in the proposed new Tamla Motown line-up.

But help was not far away as EMI's UK Division, which dealt with mostly British acts signed directly to EMI and not released through any licensing agreements, were on the lookout for new head of press – and there I was on the doorstep and they already knew how much (or how little) I would cost.

Chapter 3

CHANGING OF THE GUARD

My switch to EMI's UK Division wasn't as easy as it should have been. One of the managers wanted to hire the highly talented Moira Bellas from WEA instead of me. What he didn't know was that Moira called to tell me she'd been approached but wasn't interested. She also told me what salary she'd been offered and that, when she turned down the offer, she was going to suggest that EMI had a ready-made in-house candidate in yours truly. So between us we exercised a pincer movement which meant that, when I was finally approached, I could (albeit reluctantly) agree a deal that was cheaper than the one they had offered Bellas and the management could take credit for a deal well done. However, from our point of view it all added up to a victory for the society of press officers.

One of the things I picked up when I joined EMI was a brief history lesson of the British record business.

EMI is probably the oldest UK record company having started out as the Gramophone Company way back in 1897 with the famous HMV Dog & Trumpet logo being acquired for £100 in 1899 and first used a decade later.

In 1921 the 'Nipper' trademark was used on the first HMV

shop which opened in London's Oxford Street. In 1931 the Gramophone Company merged with the Columbia Graphophone Company to create Electrical & Music Industries - EMI – and in the same year Abbey Road Studios was opened by composer and conductor Sir Edward Elgar, who ten years earlier had opened the first HMV store. Although artists were signed to the EMI company, their records were released on HMV, Columbia or Parlophone, a German company acquired in 1927. In 1969 the Harvest label was launched as an outlet for the new 'progressive' wave of artists but it wasn't until 1972 that the first record was issued on a label bearing the name EMI – and that honour went to T.Rex.

The company also boasted an extraordinary history of major classical artists dating back to the days of Elgar and on to Sir Thomas Beecham, Yehudi Menuhin, Maria Callas, Elizabeth Schwarzkopf, Dame Janet Baker, Andre Previn, Daniel Barenboim, Riccardo Muti plus Sir Simon Rattle and Nigel Kennedy. And alongside these classical luminaries, there were a host of what were dubbed Middle of the Road artists. They were the responsibility of a separate MOR division which meant that my office had no dealings with the likes of Max Boyce, Windsor Davies and Don Estelle, Manuel & his Music of the Mountains (actually band leader Geoff Love), Berni Flint or the Wurzels, who were all hit makers.

By the time I moved over to the EMI 'pop' division, acts such as Cliff Richard, the Shadows, Helen Shapiro, Alma Cogan, Adam Faith, Manfred Mann, Frank Ifield, The Temperance Seven, The Beatles (and a host of Liverpool artists too numerous to name), the Hollies, the Animals, Dave Clark Five, Pink Floyd, Benny Hill, Pilot, Steve Harley and Queen had all topped the charts. But despite all this success, EMI was a hugely conservative, somewhat old fashioned, bureaucratic and tight-fisted (they would say careful) company with a hefty sprinkling of long-term managers not prone to a lot of risk taking. They were successful at signing artists mainly because of their size and position in a market which, until the arrival of the new breed of independents in the early 1970s, was dominated by EMI, Decca, Philips, Pye and American giants such as CBS, RCA and the Atlantic and Warner operations.

In their Manchester Square offices, EMI maintained a petty cash office and a record library, but in order to get either an advance against expenses or an album to send to a reviewer you had to get a docket signed by a suitably senior manager. And the opening times for both ran roughly along banking hours – nothing before 10am or after 4pm or at lunch time.

However, there was, as is always the case, a way round the rules and it involved concert tickets ... and as head of press I had access to them. A pair of tickets for Cliff or the Shads would usually persuade cashier Vic or library manager Jo to bend the rules and pass over some dosh or an LP after hours. The company's transport manager George could be suitably persuaded to move you up the queue for a company car on the promise of tickets to something, although I had to suffer a Morris Marina and a Triumph something or other before moving up to a flashy red Capri and then a gold Granada. And as EMI was British, the cars had to be too – other than the German-made Fords of course.

The level of bureaucracy within EMI in the mid-seventies rivalled the best that either the civil service or the BBC could offer. While petty cash and sample records were only released within set times, cars, offices and salaries were controlled by a bizarre grading system which ran either from one up to 11 or from 11 down to one – I never did work it out – and decided the size of your office, your salary level and type of company car. There was very little room for negotiation when it came to wages as the grade decided your earnings and you had to move up (or down) a grade to get an increase and that meant a bigger car and a bigger office. So there was a lot for the powers-that-be to consider. This, I realised, was why all the offices in Manchester Square were built with temporary partition walls which could be moved to make your office larger or smaller – while having a window was a whole other issue.

The man in charge of EMI Records was a Dutchman named Gerry Oord who had sold his Bovema company to EMI in exchange for a pop at the top UK job. He reported to one of the UK's music industry's true legends L.G. Wood, who had joined the company as a salesman in 1929. This was a time when all company cars had HMV number plates and, as he once told me, salesmen were required to wear a hat and carry a packet of cigarettes. "You wore a hat to be able to take it off when you greeted a retailer and you could also then offer him a cigarette."

It was Wood who officially signed off on the original Beatles deal in 1962. He also re-negotiated their deal in 1966 when, he told me, their manager Brian Epstein drove a hard bargain.

"You could never pin him down and he always had to go to the 'boys' to get their agreement. It all took so long that the new deal didn't begin until 1967 so technically they were out of contract for about six months in 1966," Wood recalled, before adding,"In those days the talks were just between me and Epstein. There were no lawyers involved until we had agreed everything."

Wood's boss, and the man at the top of the whole EMI tree, was Sir Joseph Lockwood, a Yorkshireman who saved the company from extinction in the 1950s when he went to the money men in the City of London to borrow £2 million to pay the company's wage bill.

As a lowly press officer, I had little or nothing to do with these high-ranking executives although there were the occasional run-ins. I was standing in the lift on the ground floor of Manchester Square when Alf the security guard raised a finger and beckoned in my direction. As I had no idea what he wanted, I assumed he was signalling to the very tall, slightly built, bald man standing next to me, who I looked at and said, "I think he wants you". He stared down at me and replied, "No, he wants you. Get out" That was my first encounter with Lockwood, who it turned out was not keen on sharing the lift with also-rans.

Years later, after actually getting to know Lockwood during his final years with the company, I went to his house to oversee him being filmed for an in-house archive. He was charming – and even gave me a box of fine Cuban cigars – and gained a special place in my heart when he was asked whether, after Brian Epstein's death and The Beatles split, he saw any of the 'fab four'. He said he often saw Paul and also met with John and Yoko – apparently she used to tape their meetings and lunches - before adding, without a hint of embarrassment, "I never saw the drummer or the other one." I thought 'George Harrison, this is your life' and was what you got for being the quiet Beatle.

As EMI faced up to competition from the rapidly expanding American record companies, who were now chasing UK artists, and the emerging independents, changes had to be made and one of the most significant was the hiring of a man named Bob Mercer. His long-haired image apparently didn't fit with the giant General Foods company where he was marketing executive so when offered the chance to move into the rock'n'roll business Mercer jumped in headfirst.

He embraced everything that was associated with the music business and set about changing the stuffiness that pervaded the corridors of EMI. With a set of young guns, including Paul Watts, David Munns, Nick Mobbs, Ian Groves, John Bagnall and myself, EMI became hipper, less bureaucratic and altogether a better place to be. Mercer even encouraged the often outrageous antics of TV and radio promotion man Eric ("my expenses have gone platinum") Hall.

There was however another untapped source of income for the company and it was called catalogue exploitation and this is where Bob Mercer's marketing expertise came into play. He looked at what we had in the vaults, and had access to via the licensed labels deals with the major American companies, and invested heavily in TV advertising. He took music commercials to a new level with the help of some major creative ad agencies and thanks to him a new collection of greatest hits albums appeared under the banner *20 Golden Greats*. The first seven releases between 1976 and 1978 by the Beach Boys, Glen Campbell, the Shadows, Diana Ross & the Supremes, Cliff Richard (he had 40 golden greats), Buddy Holly and Nat King Cole all went to No.1 and added considerably to the company's coffers while we collectively bathed in the reflected glory.

However, the competition was still out there and the US labels and indies came a-calling for the best people we had (including me it has to be said) and tempted them with better salaries, more attractive job titles and – most importantly – bigger and better company cars including foreign sports models. Bob Mercer had to counter this by giving people more responsibility, more opportunities and slightly better salaries ... but changing the company car policy was beyond even him.

As a press officer there were severe restrictions when it came to taking journalists to shows outside London. Staying overnight in hotels (even though EMI owned some) was a definite no-no, lunching on expenses was frowned on and sending out albums for review was closely monitored to ensure none fell into the wrong hands. But under Bob Mercer, things became freer as the company's attitude eased.

In my new role as head of the EMI Records UK press office I had a roster of hit acts that included Queen, all four solo ex-Beatles, Marc Bolan, Steve Harley, Pilot, Cliff Richard, the Shadows, Olivia Newton-John (signed for the UK only), Mr Big, plus a host of 'other' artists who came and went as their careers waned. And there was of course the multi-million selling band Pink Floyd.

Chapter 4

IN THE PINK

Roger Waters, Dave Gilmour (he was still Dave back then), Nick Mason and Rick Wright were a major EMI act and one not to be trifled with. Me and my team of four in the press office were warned by those in the Harvest label office that they could be prickly, didn't suffer fools and weren't keen on playing any record company games.

Over the years I came to see that most of those observations were true. They had stopped releasing singles in 1968, produced album artwork without any album title or band name and sent along life-size cut-outs of themselves to the reception to launch their album *Dark Side Of The Moon*. They also steadfastly refused to accept gold and platinum discs for sales or agree to photo shoots for publicity photographs and interviews were few and far between. As it turned out, being press officer for Pink Floyd was in many ways a doddle – they simply put the albums out, got rave reviews and sold bucket loads ... who needs PR?

Despite all this, in July 1975 I went to Knebworth to see Floyd play a festival that also featured fellow-Harvest artist Roy Harper (who turned up on stage with his horse

Trigger) alongside Captain Beefheart and Steve Miller plus occasional comedy moments from Monty Python's Graham Chapman. I spent a good deal of time in the green tent backstage and very little with either Floyd or Harper until I got into conversation with Gilmour. He took me up the steps on to the stage where I looked out on over 100,000 people sitting in a heat haze. It was an amazing sight but I wasn't quite dumb-struck as I managed to turn to Gilmour and mutter, "And they're all here to see you."

Cricket matches between EMI and Pink Floyd began in 1974 and went through to the nineties and I was lucky enough to feature in probably three which were played at Bradfield College and Abbey Road general manager Ken Townsend's home ground in Woburn near Marlow. I'm not sure if we ever got all four members of the band along but the Floyd side was boosted by the likes of Linda Lewis' manager Tony Gourvish, graphic designer Storm Torgersen (one of the very few spin bowlers of Norwegian descent) and guitarist Jim Cregan plus assorted crew members.

Looking back, Floyd never seemed to be jolly bandmates. There were no jokes or obvious displays of friendship towards us or each other, but back then we never thought it would end up in a legal battle between three of them and one other (Waters) about who owned the name Pink Floyd. And the passing of time doesn't seem to have made things any better between the three remaining original band members.

As befitted the band's image, the cricket matches were serious affairs with both teams dressed in regulation all white and there was always time for tea. The umpires came from the two sides and decisions on an lbw or slip catch appeal often came down to whether the band had just signed a deal or were in negotiations. If there was nothing to be gained by a 'not out' decision, then the finger was raised and Floyd's finest were dispatched to the pavilion.

A Floyd batsman is clean bowled as wicketkeeper Southall looks on

Roy Harper, Floyd's support act at Knebworth, was a long-standing EMI artist having signed to the Harvest label in 1970, but in 1977 he caused us a major problem with a song about the Watford Gap service station on the M1. Suggesting you got a "plate of grease and a pile of crap" if you ate there didn't go down well with the owners (Blue Boar) and we were forced to withdraw the track from the album and do some expensive re-pressing. The situation was not helped by the fact that one of EMI's main board directors was also on the board of Blue Boar.

There was another 'issue' in early December 1976, this time involving Floyd and the photo shoot for their forthcoming album *Animals*. The idea was to tether a large inflatable pig from the four chimney stacks of London's iconic Battersea Power Station to create the image of a flying pig.

However, things did not go to plan and for reasons still to this day never fully explained, the pig 'escaped' and flew off into the sky above London, heading in the direction of Sussex. This was where I came into the story as I took a call from the chief of the British Airports Authority who asked me if I knew anything about a big pig flying over South East England. I told him I had no idea what he was talking about and then he surprised me by asking to speak to Bob Mercer by name. I found Mercer and told him what was going on and fortunately he knew all about it as Floyd's manager Steve O'Rourke had called him earlier to tell him that there was a problem with the pig. I handed the phone over to Mercer who was told that pilots flying at around 10,000 feet into Gatwick were reporting seeing a giant pink pig in the sky. It seems that the Airport Authority's man was aware of Mercer from various newspaper reports involving EMI and the Sex Pistols (more about them later) and sensing another rock'n'roll stunt, he picked up the phone and called EMI - and got lucky first time round.

The pig eventually ran out of steam or air or hydrogen and fell to earth in a farm in Sussex much to the annoyance of a local farmer who spent some years suing Pink Floyd, claiming that the pig had scared his cows and they had stopped giving a milk which, as they were a dairy herd, was an issue. Unsurprisingly, the farmer was unsuccessful with his claim.

Roger Waters, who had dreamed up the cover shot idea of using the pig as "a symbol of hope", had to settle for album designers Hipgnosis dropping a picture of the pig into a photo of the power station. This they did expertly – and this was in the days before computer graphics, remember.

Pink Floyd's long-standing antipathy towards the media and their refusal to accommodate even journalists who were fans was there for all to see in March 1977 when I drove *Sounds* writer Hugh Fielder to the Midlands to see the band in concert at Bingley Hall. They were promoting the *Animals* album, knew we were coming but made no real attempt at bonhomie. Backstage they gave me a brief 'hello' and Fielder a cursory nod while they carried on playing darts with the crew. Whatever else they were, Floyd were never hypocrites and Fiedler had to content himself with a concert review with no insights into the minds of the Floyd

By 1983 I had moved on from my PR duties and gone through a couple of other roles at EMI before becoming head of radio and TV promotion and that brought me into contact with the now solo David Gilmour who was planning to release his album *About Face*. On the day he came into Manchester Square to meet me for lunch, the steps of the building were blocked by a gaggle of Duran Duran fans.

There was a healthy grapevine that went out from the Birmingham band's fan club telling people where the band would be during any given day – and this was a day when they were due to visit EMI. It was fascinating to stand at my office window and watch one of the true legends of rock music fight his way through a host of teenage girls who were not the least bit interested in the middle-aged and, it has to be said, slightly overweight man who fought his way into the building. There was not a hint of recognition and certainly no requests for autographs and the person most relieved by all this was Gilmour.

The next step in the plan for *About Face* involved a visit to Champneys, the luxury health farm (or resort as they preferred) together with manager Steve O'Rourke where we visited Gilmour as he prepared for his album launch and concerts.

We dined on water and salads and settled on a cover shot for the album and the track that would be the first single. But my abiding memory is, having looked at the selection of possible photos for the cover, commenting on one of Gilmour with a guitar on his lap. I said to O'Rourke that I had never seen quite such a small guitar, was it a special custom-built model? He just smiled and said, "It's a normal sized guitar, he's just got a big gut." *About Face* was eventually released with a portrait of Gilmour sans guitar, appearing to thumb a lift in a rather fetching leather jacket.

Gilmour's former Floyd bandmate Roger Waters was also delivering solo albums to EMI and in 1984 he came up with *The Pros And Cons of Hitch Hiking* which featured a Gerald Scarfe drawing of a naked girl standing on the side of the road and, coincidentally, thumbing a lift. It wasn't pretty and understandably brought a howl of protests from women's groups but despite suggestions that we draw some pants on her, Waters was adamant that the album went out as was but seemingly he didn't get his own way in America where his US record label stuck a big black box over her bum.

Over the years I was a regular visitor to Abbey Road studios. I did many of the interviews for the official history book in the studio's canteen – which was also the venue for the official author's photo of me that went on the dust jacket – or in studios with artists such as the Hollies, McCartney, Sky's Herbie Flowers, Kate Bush and sixties star Helen Shapiro. I also went to some sessions for promotion or marketing meetings but why my last get-together with Floyd's Gilmour was in there, I don't know.

In June 1988 I had been in France for the band's concert in the grounds of the Palace of Versailles, which followed a guided tour of the chateau in the company of Nick Mason and his wife and I remember that we were shown some of the rooms and private royal hideaways which weren't part of the usual tourist trail.

The show was a spectacular event with fireworks and a lavish after-show barbeque but those of us who turned up during the day in summer shirts were freezing by the time it got to midnight and beyond. Three months later the band were in Abbey Road mixing their live album *Delicate Sound of Thunder* and I met with Gilmour, but I can't for the life of me remember why I was there. Nevertheless, I realised that being in the studio with Pink Floyd was a rare moment to be cherished so I sat and listened as Gilmour re-mixed some of his live guitar work from the shows recorded in New York in August. During our conversation we, not unnaturally, touched on the subject of music and The Beatles in particular. Gilmour was a fan and started to pick out a Lennon & McCartney composition on an acoustic guitar before turning to me and asking me to "name that tune". I knew it, I knew I knew it but I couldn't get the title to come to the front of my brain and, while I could blame it on Gilmour's playing, it was more down to me being deaf or dumb ... or both.

My final meeting with one of Floyd was, bizarrely, in the men's toilet at the Natural History Museum. It was an HMV charity event with dinner served beneath the huge Diplodocus (a dinosaur skeleton nicknamed Dippy) in the main hall and among the guests was Nick Mason, the band's longtime drummer. As we stood at separate urinals, he looked over, recognised me, and as we reflected on the people who had left EMI that he once worked with, he commented, "We must be the only people still there, everybody else seems to have got out and left us behind."

Promoting rock giants like Pink Floyd was a challenge that left a legacy. But there were less successful but equally interesting bits of the business that provided very different challenges. While the American licensed labels Motown, Elektra Asylum and MCA left to go independent, EMI did link up with a number of small British labels which delivered some interesting and BOTH successful and unsuccessful artists. Red Bus brought soul singer Jesse Green, for whom I did the (free) voice-over on a series of radio commercials, while Mountain had rock group Nazareth. There was also Target Records who had signed sixties hit makers Marmalade, guitar hero Duane Eddy, the Nolan Sisters and – best of all – Adam (Batman) West.

He issued a single entitled (perhaps not surprisingly) 'Batman & Robin' and somehow I was involved in promoting it as, presumably, Target had no press officer. The stunt we worked out was to take West out onto the front of Selfridges store next to the landmark clock. Standing up there – about 30 feet above Oxford Street – was when he told me that he wasn't great with heights. He did look down a couple of times as photographers called to him but he wasn't a happy bunny (or bat). And then he told me some secret stuff about Robin which – kapow, zap, boom - must remain secret.

Retreat Records brought with them Chas & Dave and we worked on this dynamic duo from day one and, in addition to arriving in my office usually unannounced to open the fridge and enjoy one of my fine Havana cigars (I had managed to convince management that the basic elements of good PR were a good supply of booze and a cigar box), they were among the most joyous artists I ever worked with.

We had receptions on HMS Belfast and at Cook's Pie & Mash shop in Dalston where the manager gave Chas, Dave and myself lessons in how to catch hold of a live eel. They were stored in large trays with a hosepipe constantly pouring water over them and the trick, so it turned out, was to catch them behind the head (or ears if they had any). But sadly we were a trio of incompetents as eel after eel slithered out of our grasp and writhed about on the floor.

However, the duo didn't end up empty handed when, along with drummer Micky Burt, they visited the United Biscuits factory and played live on their UBN (United Biscuits Network) radio station which broadcast 24 hours a day to factories in West London, Manchester and Liverpool. At the end of it all, Chas & Dave were a bit miffed not to have been given at least a few packets of free biccies and carried on moaning as they packed their gear into the van. That was when Micky Burt told them not to worry as he had "sorted it" and he opened up a couple of drum cases which were packed with an assortment of UB's finest, including ginger nuts, hobnobs, chocolate digestives and even a few Jaffa cakes. How, when and where Burt had collected his haul remained a secret.

One of the more tedious tasks that came with running a press office was the regular mail out of records for review. It involved stuffing records in stiff-backed envelopes, sticking on address labels and lugging them down to the post room for delivery. Obviously, we focussed on the music papers and the national newspapers alongside some of the leading regional publications and a bunch of notable freelance writers. However, we did not service either the *Jewish Chronicle*, the *Catholic Herald* or *War Cry*, but did send records to *Gay News* and *Men Only* which was part of the self-styled 'King of Soho' Paul Raymond's porn empire.

Men Only was based in Raymond's Windmill Theatre and run by editor Neville Player who approached me about running a record column in the 'nudie' magazine which boasted a sizeable readership. I thought we'd give it a try and I was invited on one occasion to take some albums and visit the magazine's office at the top of the famous theatre. On the way up the winding staircase I ran into a number of topless ladies who were making their way to the stage area for a lunchtime show. They spied the albums and tried to persuade me to pass them over as they got closer and closer to me on the narrow stairway. However, my resolve was stiff and I managed to reject all offers and get up to Neville Player's offices where he showed me the design department, the photo studio and introduced me to the people who wrote some of the reader's letters. The thing that surprised me most was the number of ladies involved in the creation of a girlie mag. Despite claiming a readership of 400,000, I was never convinced that anybody actually bought *Men Only* for the record reviews.

Chapter 5

JOHN, PAUL, GEORGE, RINGO AND ME

Like most people I grew up as a Beatles fan, but even through my years of employment on *Melody Maker* and *Disc*, I'd never actually met any of them. However, that all changed in 1975. Although each of the solo Beatles was still signed to EMI they didn't come under my radar as John Lennon was in America, both Paul McCartney and Ringo Starr used independent PR people while George Harrison had little or no contact with the company. Jimmy McCulloch from Wings was the closest we got when he came in to woo one of the girls in my office and sadly he was often the worse for wear. It was no surprise when he died in 1979 aged just 26.

Even though he was in ensconced in New York, John Lennon took an interest in what we were doing with his albums *Rock'n'Roll* and *Shaved Fish* and sent postcards and telegrams - mainly to Bob Mercer who he dubbed "Bob Have Mercy On Us" - advising us on marketing ideas and chastising us when both albums failed to hit the top spot in the UK. They were amusing, slightly acerbic and I think somewhat tongue-in-cheek but were a part of Lennon's long history of sending postcards to his family, friends and, obviously, business contacts. He rarely showed any concern for record company rules and regulations and I was involved in a weird scenario in around 1976 when I was called by L.G. Wood's secretary with the instruction to make my way to his office.

This was a man I had never actually met but was aware of as the company's senior music man and being called to his office was akin to a visit to the headmaster's study. When I got there, he was holding a copy of the *New Musical Express* and pointed out something that had been written by the paper's Fred Dellar.

Whether it was a reader's letter, a piece about charity albums or Beatles tracks being available (or not) on compilation albums, I don't recall but it mentioned a charity album in aid of the World Wildlife Fund entitled *No One's Gonna Change Our World* and on it, alongside tracks by Bruce Forsyth, Spike Milligan, the Hollies and Cilla Black, was a song by The Beatles called 'Across The Universe'. Wood was concerned that Lennon had simply given the charity permission to use the track without any agreement from EMI or even the other three ex-Beatles. With that in mind, I was dispatched to find a copy of the album. So, after calling Dellar to find out where I might find a copy, I was driven by Wood's driver (in the MD's luxury saloon) to Covent Garden where I found the album which I handed over to the driver who then passed it on to Wood. A few minutes later, the driver came to find me and told me that Wood wanted to see me in his office. When I got there, he had the album on his desk and asked me if I had paid for it and had I got a receipt. When I said yes, he asked how much it was and then proceeded to give me the cash from his own pocket. However, in all the to-ing and fro-ing, I hadn't actually looked at the album and it was only later that I realised what a bizarre situation it was.

The album was issued in December 1969 - five months before The Beatles album *Let It Be*, including the track 'Across The Universe', came out - which was what seemed to rankle with Wood who obviously didn't recall (or know) that the WWF charity album had in fact been released on EMI's own Regal Starline six years earlier. To this day I don't know what happened or if anyone at EMI had given permission but I was sure it would have been the last thing Lennon would have bothered to check before giving his support to a good cause.

John Lennon was living in New York when his contract with EMI expired in the mid-seventies and both Len Wood and Bob Mercer attempted to persuade him to sign a new solo deal with the company but to no avail. In fact Mercer showed (and gave) me a copy of the letter Lennon had sent to Wood, as MD of EMI Records in early 1976, turning down an offer from the company.

In September 1975, in advance of the release of his album *Extra Texture*, George Harrison decided he would talk to one man about his music and life. The interviewer, Ray Coleman, had been on *Melody Maker* during the heady days of the sixties and travelled with The Beatles and a decade later was top dog as editor of the paper he loved so much that he named his two sons Mark and Miles (MM).

I sat in on the interview which took place at Harrison's Dark Horse Records office in the trendy Kings Road. It was there that Harrison, when asked by Coleman what it was like to be an ex-Beatle, replied that he was not keen on being an ex-anything but added "I'd rather be an ex-Beatle than an ex-Nazi." Interview over, Coleman left and

Harrison, his driver/minder and myself made our way back to Manchester Square for a meeting, but not before Harrison went to the toilet. While he used the gents on the ground floor of Manchester Square, I went upstairs to tell Bob Mercer that Harrison was on his way.

March 1976: John Lennon turns down EMI's best offer for a new deal

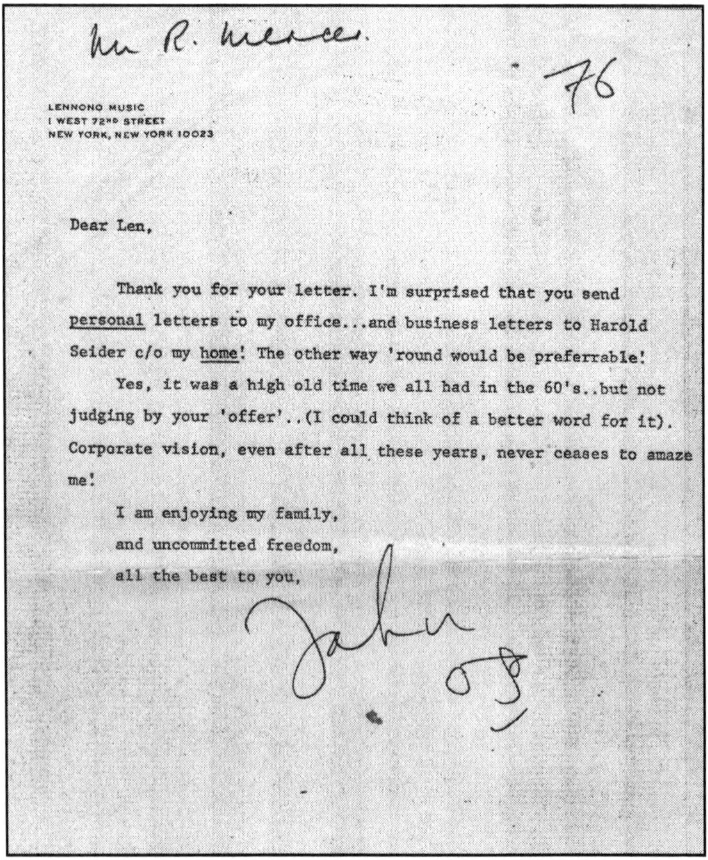

LENNONO MUSIC
1 WEST 72ND STREET
NEW YORK, NEW YORK 10023

Dear Len,

Thank you for your letter. I'm surprised that you send personal letters to my office...and business letters to Harold Seider c/o my home! The other way 'round would be preferrable!

Yes, it was a high old time we all had in the 60's..but not judging by your 'offer'..(I could think of a better word for it). Corporate vision, even after all these years, never ceases to amaze me!

I am enjoying my family,
and uncommitted freedom,
all the best to you,

On the landing where The Beatles stood for their first album cover photograph, I met Gerry Oord, the boss of EMI Records UK, who was a keen star-spotter (he was often called something much worse) and, on hearing that there was a former Beatle in the building, was on the lookout. And there I was standing before him, with hair down to my shoulders and a full beard, and he greeted me with "Hello George. Good to meet you" before asking. "What is it like working without the other Beatles?" That was when it dawned on me – he thinks I'm George Harrison.

Now it has to be said that Oord had a reputation for not recognising or knowing the acts signed to his company. The story went that when presenting a silver disc to Roy Wood at the Magic Circle, he called Ron Wood to the stage to collect the prize. Then, when people hastily shouted, "It's Roy" he apparently said "Ron Roy." A little later, at some industry do, he was talking to the boss of a rival record company who had to introduce him to two members of EMI's chart topping group Pilot. I wasn't there on either occasion but they were stories that were part of the company's folklore.

But here I was facing my boss who thinks I'm a former Beatle. As he was foreign, I took the usual British way out, and shouted at him. "Me no George, he wee wee. Me Brian Southall, your press officer." And all he said was "very good" before shaking my hand and wandering off. My next move was to find Bob Mercer before Harrison arrived for the meeting to discuss his album. I told him that if Oord was coming to the meeting with Harrison then I couldn't attend. When he asked me why, I had to explain, "Because he thinks I'm George Harrison". Then I told him the whole story, adding that if Oord asks about any press plans, he might just address the question to Harrison.

Fortunately, I was allowed to sit it out until Oord got

bored and left, and then I joined in and related the whole sorry tale to Harrison who thought it was hilarious. I later learned that he went back to Apple and told all the staff there about the day when a two-bit press officer was mistaken for a multi-million rock legend by the boss of his record company.

Soon after that incident, Harrison left EMI for good with some suggesting that his departure was more to do with EMI having a Defence Division (they made things that you defended with rather than attacked, apparently) than Oord's big booboo or the end of his contract.

Still in contract with EMI, Ringo Starr was an occasional visitor to Manchester Square but spent very little time with anybody other than Bob Mercer. So it was Paul McCartney who became the focus of the company's attention. My dealings with him began after I became a marketing manager somewhere in late 1977 as 'Mull of Kintyre' came out and dominated the singles chart for weeks on end.

When McCartney first played the track to a bunch of us there were some serious concerns voiced about the record's commercial appeal, but Macca knew best and he proved us all wrong, including the telephone sales girls based in the EMI factory at Hayes. On a weekly basis, we so-called marketing know-alls played new singles to this team whose job it was to call up the major UK record dealers and sell them our hottest new releases. The girls were handed voting cards with the words 'hit' and 'miss' printed on them and they held them up to register their opinion of a record. The unanimous vote on 'Mull of Kintyre' (and one other record we'll to come later) was 'miss' with some of the sassier young ladies holding the two cards together to spell out 'shit'. So then we knew… but once again the artist and the British public proved us wrong.

On the back of the extraordinary success of his Christmas No.1 - and unaware of the factory girls' 'review' - McCartney and wife Linda paid a visit to our offices and went on a sort of royal tour, meeting and greeting those of us who played some small part in the record's success. When he popped into my cramped corner office, he spotted a sizable wall clock featuring a sci-fi drawing of a giant robot and the four members of Queen as they appeared on the cover of their album *News Of The World.* McCartney asked what they were and when I told him we gave them away to media to promote the album, he wanted to know why we hadn't done some sort of giveaway for him. I could only tell him "you didn't ask."

Paul and Linda McCartney spend time with me (left) and EMI boss Rupert Perry (right)

By 1983, I had become head of corporate PR for EMI and was heavily involved with the BRIT Awards where one of my tasks was getting our nominated artists to attend on the off-chance they had won something. I don't think any of The Beatles had ever attended and it was down to me to try and get McCartney along. He was a nominated artist on the back of his No.1 album *Tug of War.* The event's organisers, the British Phonographic Industry (BPI), were keen to get the great man along so it was left to me to call up the offices of MPL (McCartney Productions Limited) based in London's Soho Square and explain how great it would be if Paul came along.

When I was asked the question, "What's he won?" I had to reply that I didn't know details of any winners as that was a well-kept secret. After being told that McCartney didn't attend events where he hadn't won something, the next thing I heard was the repeated question, "So what's he won?"

With that in mind I went back to the BPI, explained the situation and was then able to call MPL and confirm that McCartney's name would appear on the winner's list. And he was there at the Dorchester Hotel in February 1983 when he collected the award as Best British Male Artist and also received a special Sony Award for Technical Excellence.

Funny how these things work out and that was also the night I met Michael Jackson, so it was a memorable evening for me too. We gave McCartney a table for the awards ceremony and one of his guests was Jackson and when I went over to say hello to Paul, he asked if I knew Michael. I said we had met briefly, years ago along with his brothers, when the Jackson 5 played *The Talk of the Town* but it was an occasion that Michael – surprise, surprise - didn't seem to recall.

Three years before McCartney's BRIT successes, his Liverpool pal and song-writing partner John Lennon was shot in New York on December 8 1980 and, as head of PR for EMI, I was on the receiving end of a very early morning phone call to tell me the news. One of the security guys at Manchester Square - Bob it was - called me at home and said he was being inundated with phone calls from the media in all its forms. I left my home about 30 miles away from London, drove into the office and set about creating and issuing a statement of sympathy and sadness while also collecting comments from those people who had been closely connected with John – former EMI chairman Sir Joseph Lockwood, retired managing director L.G. Wood and Abbey Road manager Ken Townsend.

Most of that extraordinary day was then spent fielding calls from the media as they searched for information and comments plus details of our plans concerning Lennon's recordings, both with The Beatles and as a solo artist. What none of them realised was that no Beatles or Lennon records had ever been deleted from our catalogue so we re-issued nothing but just re-pressed things as the demand grew.

It was a weird and hugely sad time not helped by one of our finest 'heavyweight' Sunday papers calling to ask if we would do a deal with them and offer all John's recordings to their readers at a special price --- I gave them a resounding NO!

The renewed interest in the single 'Imagine' also brought about calls from parents whose children (presumably too young to buy the record in 1975) had bought 'Imagine' in the aftermath of John's death only to discover that the B-side 'Working Class Hero' included the word f******. One mother was particularly annoyed that we hadn't censored or re-recorded it before putting it out again. It required me to point out that the record was the original version John recorded in 1970 and that he was now dead for Christ's sake. Not very diplomatic but Lennon's death was a tragedy not just for me but for all music lovers. He remained the only Beatle I never met and while I would not have expected him to be Mr. Charming (I'd heard stories about his sarcasm and cruel wit), I was disappointed that the plans we had for a welcome home 'do' whenever he came back to the UK would never materialise.

On the 40th anniversary of Lennon's murder I was invited to recall that day and write an article for the *Daily Telegraph's* colour magazine which appeared with a small photo of me and, rather creepily, a larger one of Lennon signing his autograph for his killer.

After Lennon's death I did spend some time with his widow Yoko Ono - once on the phone (embarrassing) and once over lunch (much better).

Sometime in the eighties EMI's video arm put together a collection of Lennon's work which included music videos and concert footage and I was asked to write the sleeve notes. This involved me chatting to Yoko on the phone to get some details and background, and my only recollection of the conversation is of me trying desperately to avoid saying the words "live" or "shot" when talking about Lennon as, of course, he wasn't alive and had been shot.

Yoko was both very understanding and gracious and went to some lengths to put me at ease. I joined her some time later when she and son Sean Lennon attended a fancy lunch in one of London's Park Lane hotels to accept and unveil a statue of Lennon which HMV record stores had commissioned.

She was again charming but I noticed that she was ever-watchful of her teenage son who was the centre of attention with the waitresses and female lunch guests – and seemed to be very much enjoying the moment.

Sean Lennon (left), Yoko Ono, me, and (far right) PR guru Rob Goldstone at the unveiling of HMV's John Lennon statue

With Lennon's demise and both Harrison and Starr no longer recording for EMI, we were left with McCartney and that was never without its moments. In late 1983 we released the single 'Say Say Say' which featured McCartney and his new best buddy Michael Jackson and it was down to my TV and radio promotion team to get the record played and the video shown all around the country. Radio play was not a problem but in order to get on to the various TV shows – McCartney was not going to perform live – there had to be a video and that was where the problems started.

There was a sort of unofficial midweek singles chart which came out on a Friday and gave people like Michael Hurll, producer of *Top of The Pops*, an idea of the records moving up which he might want to feature on the following week's show. With 'Say Say Say' showing at No.3, Hurll was keen to know what we had from McCartney that he could use. At that stage we had no video as nothing had come from MPL despite assurances that it was "on its way." Hurll had been badly burned by the Rolling Stones' video for their single 'Undercover of The Night' which he had used on a show apparently without actually seeing it. The problem? The violent shootouts and ultimate shooting of Mick Jagger's character.

After being embarrassed by the Stones – and presumably hauled over the BBC's hottest coals - Hurll insisted on having all videos under consideration delivered to him by the Tuesday before the show's final editing on Wednesday for broadcast on Thursday. That was the deadline we were working with on 'Say Say Say' and when that news was reported to McCartney's office, we were again assured that a video would arrive before the Tuesday deadline.

And did it? Did it hell. Despite the record being in the chart at No.3, Hurll was unable to feature it as there was no video. And that, apparently, sent McCartney (who I think, finally delivered his video some time on Wednesday) into a tail-spin. His office called me up to tell me that McCartney was not happy and wanted me fired. When I asked "why?" I was told it was because I/we had failed to get his video on *Top of the Pops* and this was despite me pointing out that this was the video we didn't have.

When I asked his manager where he stood in the argument, he said, "I'll be the first cab off the rank." I asked why and he simply explained, "Because I let you f*** it up." Now it was McCartney's turn to spring into action and calls were made to high-ranking execs at the BBC - people who wouldn't take my call if I was on fire - to get some sort of coverage on the telly. It ended up with McCartney going onto Noel Edmonds Saturday night *Late Late Breakfast Show* (a show that never used videos) and introducing the video but not being very forthcoming in the interview. I was told that he wasn't a fan of Edmonds for some reason but needs must when an artist wants some promo time.

This show was aired on Saturday evening after most of the record shops in the UK had closed - and their singles sales had already been logged for the following week's chart - so there was no guarantee that the record would go up from three. In fact, it dropped to nine but on the back of airplay and McCartney getting his video on Edmonds' show, it shot back up to No.2 where it peaked and became McCartney's fifth single that missed the top spot by one place. The last word I heard from MPL was that McCartney was saying: "do I have to do everything around here?"

Actually we had quite a good relationship with MPL to the extent that they often told us when McCartney was coming up from his home in Sussex and then having a car take him to his office in Soho Square. If there was a new record out and we had a poster campaign running, we then made sure that the route from Victoria to Soho was well plastered with fly posters for the great man's new release. This mostly illegal advertising (we made sure that there were no references to EMI or MPL on the posters) was done by 'Terry the Pill', who actually charged us VAT although I'm not sure how he (or we) got away with it.

One of my last McCartney moments (you will gather that he hadn't got me fired) came in Liverpool in November 1984 when his film *Give My Regards To Broad Street* was premiered in his home city. I was deputed by my boss to represent EMI at this gala event when the great and good of Liverpool - members of various sixties groups, footballers from the city's two teams and assorted official luminaries - gathered at the Odeon cinema where usherettes formed a guard of honour with raised torches for Mr & Mrs McCartney.

My abiding memory of the night, having sat through 13 minutes of *Rupert And The Frog Song* (including the 'Frog Chorus') and then *Give My Regards To Broad Street*, was the film's climax where McCartney phones to say that he has found what he had lost (sorry if this is a plot spoiler). At that point somebody from the roped-off VIP area shouted quite loudly (and in a strong Scouse accent) "Thank f*** for that, can we go home now?"

During the 1970s I was involved in the release of some questionable Beatles compilation albums *with Rock 'N' Roll Music, The Beatles At The Hollywood Bowl, Love Songs* and *Beatles Ballads* among them, but the upside was that these collections - particularly *Hollywood Bowl* and *Rock 'N' Roll Music* - meant I got to meet George Martin. He was involved with these two releases - not always to his satisfaction it has to be said - but I was more interested in talking to the man often called the "fifth Beatle" although it was a title he never claimed or relished. My abiding personal memory is of the day when I was walking close to Manchester Square and heard this shout of "Brian, Brian" and looked over to see it was Martin calling my name. The man who made the records I religiously bought in the sixties was using my first name – and inviting me to have a cup of tea with him.

Over the years George Martin and I corresponded by letter on a host of subjects including (obviously) the Beatles, my back operation and his knighthood. He also, on occasions, wrote in search of old records he had produced, including Spike Milligan's novelty record 'Girl On A Pony' which he made for Warner Bros. Records in 1972. I helped source a copy from my contacts at Warners and Martin dropped me a line in 1988.

Sir George Martin's letter of thanks for a Spike Milligan record

30th March 1998

Dear Brian,

I don't think I have thanked you enough for all your efforts to get Spike Milligan's "Girl on a Pony". I know he will be very appreciative, as it was a very special song for him.

Kind regards.

Sir George Martin, C.B.E.

Although he wasn't directly involved in The Beatles album that never was, George Martin's fingerprints were all over it. *Sessions* was a 13 track collection of unreleased Beatles tracks, produced by Martin, brought together from the Abbey Road tape archives which were stored in a secret underground vault. When they were collected, we planned to issue the set in November 1984 and my role was to pull together the artwork and write the sleeve notes.

For the front cover I chose an early black and white shot of the foursome in the car park at Abbey Road and then, for the back image, purchased the rights to a picture of four pairs of Beatles' boots, each bearing the name of a Beatle, taken by Robert Freeman in a dressing room. For the inside bag I unearthed a couple of historic, and possibly previously unseen, photos of John Lennon and George Harrison together and Paul McCartney with Ringo Starr. The negotiations for Freeman's back cover image – he was responsible for the cover artwork on the albums *With The Beatles*, *Beatles For Sale*, *Help* and *Rubber Soul* – took place with his charming wife Tiddy who, at that time, was overseeing his catalogue. We agreed a fee – quite a big one I remember – and, in addition to the rights to the 'boots shot', she kindly gave me three prints of The Beatles taken, and signed, by Freeman. As we prepared for the album's release, we contacted Apple to tell them about the plan and invite the surviving band members to get involved - change the artwork, re-mix the tracks or even add new titles - but they weren't interested. Instead they decided to stop the release with a court injunction, claiming that some of the tracks were incomplete and others were never intended for commercial release.

We lost the case and the album, for which I suggested the phrase "*1,2,3,4*" as a title (it was a phrase every band used to open a song), was never officially released, although pretty soon a bootleg version was on the market and that brought a different problem down on my head.

Together with two of EMI's legal executives and a representative from Camden Trading Standards, we visited London's Camden Market one Saturday morning to see if we could find what we were looking for. And sure enough there was a copy of the bootleg *Sessions* album with the same tracks but with a brash coloured collage cover design, a different selection of photographs, both EMI and Parlophone logos, appropriate © copyright dates and credits for George Martin as original producer and Geoff Emerick for remixing.

There was also a credit for me and my colleague Mike

Heatley (albeit spelt wrongly) for compilation and picture research plus sleeve notes with my name at the bottom as the author. I had written sleeve notes for the official album but they were not these. However, as my name was on them, there were those at Apple who wanted my head on a stake. My boss Mercer had to show Apple's Neil Aspinall my original sleeve notes to get me off the hook (or stick) and when they finally accepted that the whole thing was an illegal bootleg album – for which they would get no royalties – they backed off.

We all had our suspicions as to who, from within EMI's global organisation, had leaked the tapes which had been sent out to various territories in readiness for release but no prosecution or firing followed and The Beatles did ultimately include many of the *Sessions* tracks on their three *Anthology* albums.

Bringing things up to date, nearly 40 years on from the proposed release of the *Sessions* LP - 'the album that never was' made a surprise appearance at a music memorabilia auction in Chippenham, Wiltshire in August 2023. It seems that someone, who had almost certainly worked for EMI back in the day, had kept copies of the original proposed front sleeve design, an internal memo, a draft press release, a helpful list of questions and answers about the album together with a selection of black and white and colour photos.

All this material had originally been put together by me in December 1984 - we had by then pushed the release date into 1985 - and was distributed to EMI companies around the world for them to use whenever the album came out. It was almost, but not quite, the finished article and looking back at the items in the auctioneer's catalogue, I don't think I did a bad job.

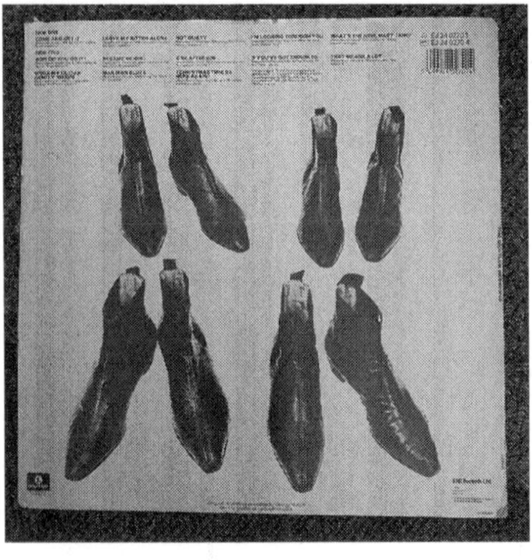

The cover of The Beatles' Sessions album that never came out but was later auctioned plus the bootleg version that came out with a different coloured cover shot

But what struck me as odd was a mention I had made in the memo about one of the colour transparencies used in the press kit which was taken by Michael Cooper during the 1967 *Sgt Pepper* cover photo shoot. It was an alternative to the chosen back cover image on the original sleeve of the Beatles with their backs to the camera and shows Paul McCartney in profile which, I pronounced, disproved a theory that McCartney was not at the session and that roadie Mal Evans had stood in for him. Author Neville Stannard in his book *The Long And Winding Road*, had suggested that McCartney had fallen out with the other Beatles and gone off to America and missed the shoot.

These two rare, or even never published, photos were to be used on the official Sessions album's inside bag

However, it is accepted that the photo session took place on March 30 1967 and McCartney left for the USA on April 3 - and various out-takes from the session, not seen at the time, show McCartney was there in all his full frontal glory.

Among the possible questions (and answers) I sent out for the EMI companies to use with their local media were these:

Q) Did you ask the Beatles permission to release this record - how did they react? Have they stopped its release in the past?

A) Each of the Beatles is aware of this release and we haven't received any reaction at all. As we have never suggested such a release in the past, the question of stopping its release has never arisen.

Q) Do you not think you are guilty of exploiting/ripping off the Beatles by releasing tracks that they themselves never intended for release?

A) Bootleggers and counterfeiters are guilty of ripping off the Beatles not EMI who are the legal owners of this material. An awful lot of care and consideration has gone into this project to make it a unique and interesting album.

Q) Why were these tracks not released by the Beatles at the time?

A) This is impossible to answer but one can only presume that they didn't fit into the style at the time and other tracks were considered to be better singles.

Q) What do the Beatles earn from this record?

A) The exact amounts are a matter of confidence between EMI and the Beatles but the royalty payments to the group will be in line with the contract in operation at the time of the original recording.

What was most surprising, considering there was nothing new in the proposed press pack - all the photos have been used or published since 1984 - was that the whole lot (number 993) was given a reserve price between £5000 and £7000. On the day bidding, for what was described by the auctioneer as a "fantastic item", began near the end of day two of the auction and started out at £7000. Within a few minutes it had been sold for ... wait for it ... £8000! Makes me wish I had kept copies of ALL the stuff I wrote back then.

My final run-in with The Beatles came after I had left EMI in 1989 and was working as a consultant for a rival music company. I was in their New York office, when I got a call from Adam Cooper, son of Michael Cooper who had taken the original photographs for the album *Sgt Pepper's Lonely Hearts Club Band*. We had first made contact in 1987 as EMI prepared for the release of *Sgt Pepper* on CD and we were preparing a new booklet to go with the release. Coincidentally Adam had called me to ask permission to use some of the original album artwork - which was still owned by EMI back then - in a book he was compiling of his father's work. We then agreed a deal whereby he got the images he wanted for the book and we got some of the outtakes his father had taken back in 1967. But as we entered the nineties, Apple appeared on the horizon once again with their lawyers in tow. They were suing Cooper over ownership of the outtakes, claiming that they were owned by Apple, even though The Beatles company didn't actually exist in 1967.

Nevertheless the whole thing ended up in the highest of Britain's law courts in the Strand where Cooper argued that outtakes - those images from the session, which back then was almost certainly paid for by the record company, which were not used on the record sleeve or in the marketing campaign - remained the property of the photographer. That was my understanding of things when I was asked to come back from America post-haste to appear in court and give evidence on Cooper's behalf - against Apple and The Beatles. All I could say under oath was that EMI did not claim ownership of the outtakes and there was no contract anywhere in the files that gave ownership of the outtakes to either us or The Beatles, so our presumption was that they belonged to Michael Cooper, and now formed part of the estate owned by his son.

While in the witness box, being watched all the time by Neil Aspinall who, I don't think had forgiven me over the *Sessions* affair, I tried to inject a bit of Beatles-related humour. I was asked to look at a number of large files of paperwork, or albums as they were called in court, which were of various colours. As the QC for Apple took me through a yellow album, a white album and a black album, I offered up a witty (in my eyes) line suggesting, "All we need now are the red and blue albums and we'll have a complete set." Beatles fans will understand the 'red and blue' album reference but the whole thing fell on stony ground in the High Court where the judge suggested I stick to the facts.

And the fact is, this was one of the few times that Apple lost a court case over trademarks, copyrights or ownership and Adam Cooper walked away with all his dad's *Sgt Pepper* pictures, including the ones featuring him on the set, aged just three.

Chapter 6

CLIFF'S ROCK OF AGES

When I took over as head of press for EMI's UK division one of the company's longest serving and most successful artists came as part of the package. Cliff Richard had his first hit in my first year at senior school in the late fifties but was still making records in the mid-seventies ... and he didn't hire independent PR or promotion people. He was very much our man, a company man who trusted his fate to the likes of Bob Mercer, Eric Hall and me amongst others. And we were all happy to do a job for him as he was far from the most demanding act we had and remained popular with most of the media which made our job relatively easy although there were some unforeseen 'iffy' moments.

In late 1975 Cliff decided on an American song called 'Honky Tonk Angel' as his new single but when it was released there was uproar as unbeknownst to him (or us for that matter) the phrase 'honky tonk angel' meant a prostitute in the US. It was claimed that Cliff thought it was something to do with a Chinese woman (not very woke in these days of wokeness) and when the true meaning came to light he refused to promote it.

Here I am, close at hand, during Cliff's HMV record signing session

He also made a TV appearance asking us to withdraw the single which we did eventually (probably when it failed to chart) and in the great scheme of things it really had no great impact on the company's fortunes.

This was also about the time when *New Musical Express*, who were far more interested in the likes of David Bowie, Bob Marley, Little Feat, Joni Mitchell and Led Zeppelin, printed a highly critical and, in the view of Cliff's management, potentially libellous concert review. I can't remember where the show was but I did read the article and think that it was more than a tad cruel even for the *NME*. In the end there was no legal action but Cliff's office asked us to pull all EMI advertising from the music paper for a period in protest. Despite their request, we refused, pointing out that there were other acts on the label that might benefit from ads in the *NME*.

A year - and many lunches and dinners with Cliff around the country, both before and after shows later - the USSR appeared on the horizon. Early in 1976 Cliff became the first British pop artist to have albums released in the USSR when *I'm Nearly Famous* and a *Best Of Cliff* collection were issued. And then came the call for him to perform behind the Iron Curtain.

Ahead of him travelling to Moscow, there was a bit of media frenzy about the trip to a Communist country led by Leonid Breshnev, where no recordings by Elvis Presley or The Beatles had been officially sanctioned for release. This interest included the London-office of either *Pravda* or *TASS*, the two major USSR news agencies, calling me up for an exclusive pre-tour interview with Cliff. We had already agreed with him that he was not doing any interviews in advance of him travelling to the USSR, so the answer was a polite 'No' (or 'Niet') with the added sweetener that he would happily talk to the press when he arrived. However, this was not good enough for their man in London who was very keen to make a note of my name in his book (might have been a black one, who knows) and assure me that any plans I might have to travel to the USSR in the near future would not get off the ground once he had reported back to his masters.

While I didn't travel to the USSR with (or without) Cliff, I did take a trip to Belfast with him in October 1976 when *Melody Maker's* Harry Doherty was keen to do a feature on the devout Christian singer giving a religious concert in Northern Ireland's capital city during the 'Troubles.' The fact that Doherty came from Derry (or Londonderry according to the British government) added an extra dash of interest.

However, getting the OK from EMI's powers-that-be to go to Northern Ireland in the mid-seventies made a possible trip to Moscow seem like child's play. The company's executives and insurance company were concerned that I (not Cliff Richard) might get kidnapped or injured or even killed and wondered whether I was worth the risk - or a huge ransom demand and pay out? At the end of the day, I told them that if it's OK for Cliff and Harry Doherty to go, then I was going too and they could do whatever they saw fit, which looking back was either very bolshie or bonkers. We stayed at a hotel somewhere near Stormont, the home of the Northern Ireland Parliament, and travelled into Belfast during daylight for an afternoon show (those were the rules laid down by whoever was in charge) and Cliff was accompanied by the few of his regular musicians who had volunteered to make the journey.

Belfast during the seventies was a hostile place and it struck me, as we drove through the city, that this was the first time I had ever seen fully armed British troops, tanks and armoured cars out and about as part of a UK city-scape. When we got near the hall, we were escorted into the venue by a small squad (how big's a squad?) who surrounded us, told us to walk quickly and stressed that if they said 'get down', we should drop to the ground. It was all a bit odd but the show went ahead and Doherty got his interview which appeared under the heading "Cliff Brings Good News To Belfast." The next twist in the tale was that Doherty was going to go and visit his family in Derry the next day (a Sunday), so it was left to me to while away a Saturday night watching TV (*Starsky & Hutch* and *Match Of The Day* probably) while Doherty typed up his feature in his room for me to take back and deliver to his editor at *Melody Maker* on Monday.

The next morning, I asked the hotel to call a cab to take me to Belfast Airport to catch a plane home and when it arrived the driver asked me what seemed an odd question about the route I wanted him to take, explaining that the shortest way wasn't always the quickest. I told him to go anyway he wanted, so he went the long way. I later discovered that a bomb had exploded somewhere along the short route and I presumed the word had gone out for cabs - even those carrying Englishman - to avoid the area. Belfast Airport had a strict no entry zone set up a mile or so away from the terminal where British soldiers stopped and questioned all those travelling to meet people or catch a plane.

Once through security, I sat myself in the airport café only to be disturbed by an extraordinary sound – a noise I had never heard before ... and it was getting closer. It turned out to be the crash of British soldiers' heavy army boots resounding on the airport's tiled floors and once again there was a small squad of them - but this time they were simply collecting the Sunday papers.

But that wasn't the end of my one and only trip to Belfast as Special Branch or similar had a surprise waiting for me at Heathrow Airport. As I made my way through arrivals, I was called over for a chat, mainly about why my travelling companion Harry Doherty wasn't with me and where was he? I told them he had gone to visit family in Derry (or Londonderry to them) and was coming back later in the week. Happy with that explanation, they sent me on my way and I didn't know whether to be reassured that the security service were on the ball or concerned about how much they knew about us all - who we got on planes with and why they didn't come back when they were expected. It was a story I never shared with Cliff who could have probably topped it with tales of travelling in the USSR under the scrutiny of their secret police.

During my first trip to America in 1977, after travelling with Queen on the East Coast, I flew over to Los Angeles to spend time at Capitol Records, the company bought by Sir Joseph Lockwood in 1955 for $8.5 million. And I found two familiar faces were in town at the same time. Cliff Richard had signed to Elton John's Rocket Records for releases in America and he was there promoting his album *Every Face Tells A Story* - a Top 10 hit in the UK - but sadly not any sort of a hit in the US where there was a change of cover artwork with Cliff in, what some thought to be, a rather overly 'butch' t-shirt pose. My former *Disc* colleague and boss at A&M Records, Mike Ledgerwood, was now, it turned out, living in California and had read about Cliff's visit and a concert I think in San Diego although I can't find any record of it anywhere. I was there so I know it happened. Mike Ledgerwood found me at the Beverly Wilshire Hotel and said he had spoken to the editor of *Melody Maker*, Ray Coleman, and sold him on the idea of a 'Cliff Richard in US' piece and wanted me to fix tickets for the show and an interview. This I did, via a call to Cliff's most amiable manager Peter Gormley, but, for whatever reason, Mike Ledgerwood never showed up ... and our earlier meeting in the hotel café was the last time I saw him until 2018 when we both turned up at the funeral of another former journalist colleague. I didn't think it was the time or place to ask "So what happened to you in California 40 years ago?"

There was always constant questioning by the media about Cliff's sexuality and religious beliefs and he invariably suggested that his sexuality was nobody's business but his (fair enough) and his Christianity was a well-covered subject that he was never embarrassed by -

and why should he be? But every now and again we had questions about his image and how people would react to things said and done.

I was in Paris on holiday with my wife Pat in early 1978 when Cliff's manager Peter Gormley (we often asked "why couldn't all rock managers be like him" - a gentleman who never raised his voice or lost his temper but still made his point) was also there taking a break. We met up and one thing we discussed was the proposed artwork for the cover of the album *Green Light*. It featured Cliff back-lit by a bright green light which, in some shots, made it look as though he actually had a halo. And as it wasn't a Christian album - although it was the follow-up to one that was called *Small Corners* - we had concerns that people might misconstrue what it was all about. Peter Gormley was always prepared to listen and saw, but didn't necessarily agree with, the point we were making. So compromise was the order of the day. The final cover featured Cliff with a mighty green light looming up behind him which couldn't be seen to have any religious connotations. And the album reached No. 25 in the UK chart which was a few places higher than his religious offering.

It's fair to say that Cliff did have a special place in EMI's history and with the people who worked with him – despite most of us not being the least bit religious. He was never pious or preaching and as far as I know there were never any attempts to convert any of us to his beliefs. And it has to be said he holds a special place in my list of rock stars as the best and most obliging when it comes to autographs. I've been with a few 'stars' who were more like divas and once even stood by as a young man asked a megastar "would you mind signing this" as he proffered a piece of paper and pen. The musician simply said "yes" and did nothing. The fan was bemused until it was clearly explained to him by said star, "You asked me if I'd mind signing this and I would." At this point the rock star's wife nudged him and told him not to be so difficult and just sign. And he did as he was told.

Cliff's always happy to sign for a fan ... or for a man from the record company

I've been with Cliff in airports, hotels and even restaurants where people have come up to him mid-course and he always seemed happy to oblige. Fortunately, it was before the age of 'selfies' or we'd never have got to pudding.

One of the dinners where he wasn't confronted by fans was a private affair at a swanky London hotel in 1979 when we celebrated his 21 years with EMI and where we gave him the 'key' to Manchester Square. Four years later we celebrated his 25 years in the music business with another fancy dinner in another posh hotel but I can't remember what, if anything, we gave the man who probably has everything.

What we did do, however, involved me arranging for a special 25th anniversary photograph to be taken by Lord Snowdon, the celebrated photographer and ex-husband of Princess Margaret.

It meant me spending a good part of the day at Snowdon's fancy studio where he was surrounded by attractive, very well spoken young gals from fine backgrounds who dashed around getting everything in order for 'his Lordship'.

In all honesty, he wasn't the warmest or nicest man I've ever met and, after a few attempts at conversation, I left him to get on with his picture taking while Cliff posed professionally.

The idea was to pick the best shot and get a limited number reproduced and framed with each one bearing Snowdon's name and Cliff's signature. We ordered up 75 which we gave away to the top radio and TV executives, producers and presenters plus major retailers. As the instigator of the plan, I felt it only fitting and fair for me to have number 1/75 for my personal collection and nobody seemed to mind ... or know.

Thinking back, it's odd that we didn't perhaps have more of these anniversary moments for long-serving artists. Certainly Paul McCartney would have qualified with his more than fifty years, as would the Shadows who joined way back in the late fifties and stayed for at least 20 years and both would probably have appreciated the gesture. And then there's Pink Floyd, stalwarts since 1967 and still there in 2015 but you can be pretty confident that they wouldn't have shown up for a fancy dinner or posed for a celebratory photo session. If I remember rightly they would never accept gold or platinum records for sales of their albums and they certainly never approved any glossy 8x10 press shots to go with their records.

The coveted copy No 1 of the Cliff Richard print signed by both Lord Snowdon and Cliff

Despite his long and hugely successful career, Cliff Richard has, in my mind, made at least a couple of professional errors in his time at the top.

Firstly in 1986 he opted to star in *Time*, a sci-fi musical co-written by sixties pop idol Dave Clark (he of the DC Five), recorded and released as an album by EMI and, I believe, we might even have pumped some cash into the project. I saw it at least three times in the company of various company executives. However, few, if any of them, lasted the full course as they made their excuses and left.

To my mind it was far from the best thing I had seen on a London stage but surprisingly (to me at least) it ran for two years despite some poor reviews, including one that suggested it was "the most sensational contrast between mountainous spectacle and molehill content the musical theatre goer has seen."

Ten years later, by which time I had stopped working with Cliff, the great man chose to put on, co-write and appear in *Heathcliff*, a musical adaptation of Emily Bronte's *Wuthering Heights* which ended up at the Hammersmith Odeon in February 1997.

Despite music by John Farrar (an ex-Shadow) and lyrics by Tim Rice, it was mauled by the critics who called it, "living dull", "withering heights rather than wuthering heights" and a "wretched show."

Even so, the show broke box office records and ran for five months - longer even than Cliff had planned - and, courtesy of free tickets from his office, I went to see it with my wife plus some friends who were huge Cliff fans - he could do no wrong in their eyes.

It was, to put it kindly, an all-round disappointing evening's entertainment, but when we got together backstage and after hugs, Cliff asked me what I thought, I very convincingly, and with a straight face, told him "I've never seen anything like it." And I hadn't, but fortunately he took it the wrong way – as a compliment!

And I haven't seen or spoken to him since but hopefully that's more to do with circumstances than anything I said.

Chapter 7

ANY OTHER EMI BUSINESS

Forever on the lookout for new acts to sign and hopefully break, EMI Records always boasted a sizeable roster of acts covering pop, rock, MOR and classical but in the mid-seventies we signed a host of artists to try and make up for the loss of American stars who departed when their labels left EMI to set up their own operations in the UK. Some cynics described it as a policy based on the principle of "if you threw enough shit at the wall, some of it must stick."

Some that did stick and are worthy of a mention are Marshall Hain, Mr Big, Be Bop Deluxe and a band signed to our Australian company called Little River Band who were a fun bunch and made some good records. I travelled to Hamburg with them in October 1976 and took with me *NME* writer David Hepworth, who was at that time a freelance journalist and a sales assistant in the HMV shop in Oxford Street, and my wife. Hepworth met the band, we watched the show and then it was off to the seedy area of Hamburg known as the 'red light district.'

We were walking where The Beatles (and a host of other British bands) had no doubt gone before but this time the arrangement was that band members took it in turns to stay with my wife as the others went in shifts to take a peek at the goods on offer. While they had no hits in the UK, LRB did notch up ten Top 20 hits in America and a couple of hit albums but for all their good music, the thing that made the biggest impact on me (and on Hepworth as he used the quote in his feature) was drummer Derek Pellici's description of life as a shit sandwich ..."the more bread you have, the less shit you eat."

LRB were among a long list of acts released on the EMI label as opposed to HMV, Parlophone or Harvest, but despite the company dating back to the 1930s, there wasn't an actual EMI label on any records until 1972. Before I joined, the company used those three famous imprints plus Columbia but Gerry Oord, the man who thought I was George Harrison, was the brains behind the EMI label. The first time the new label appeared in the charts was on T Rex's 'Metal Guru' in 1972 and over the years Marc Bolan was a regular and entertaining visitor to the offices. He usually came in his best sparkly gear and platform boots and when we asked about the next record and what it would sound like, he would happily - and without any fear of being done for plagiarism - tell us things like, "There's a bit of 'Wild Horses' and something from *Abbey Road*." And if there was, we never actually spotted it. His death, at the age of 29, in a car crash was a sad day for all of us and at his funeral at Golders Green Crematorium, we joined the likes of David Bowie, Rod Stewart, Steve Harley and producer Tony Visconti to say goodbye to a glam rock legend who was also a friend.

After T Rex, acts such as Cliff Richard, the Shadows, Pilot, Steve Harley, Queen and even American singer Andy Williams, who signed to EMI in 1984, all notched up hits on the 'new' orange and red EMI label as the Columbia imprint was gradually phased out. One of the other bands to make an appearance on the EMI label in 1974 were a prog rock outfit called Druid who, we hoped, might appeal to fans of our very own dear Pink Floyd. As Floyd had been almost entirely absent from the UK tour circuit between 1973 and 1977, there was a thought that Druid might fill the gap and the fact that they were produced by Bob Harris, host of *The Old Grey Whistle Test* TV show (on which they appeared), meant, in our minds, that we had it made. But, as with the best laid plans, it fell apart as both their albums failed to chart and by 1977 they had broken up.

Andy Williams posing with me during his time with EMI in 1984

Ultimately, EMI switched the HMV label, which was first used on records in the 1890s and as the brand for record stores in the 1920s, to become its major classical imprint although former Smiths' frontman Morrissey insisted on using it when he signed to EMI and he took it back into the charts in 1988 for the first time in 16 years.

There was some logic in what we tried to do back then to break new acts - it wasn't all 'suck it and see'. We had regular A&R, marketing and promotion meetings to discuss and debate new signings and releases. Of course the A&R men (and they were all men) sometimes threw a spanner in the works by demanding that records by acts they had signed were released despite any resistance from the rest of us. After all, they had signed them to the company on the promise that the records they made would be released and sometimes discs were issued just to keep some people happy.

We were full of good ideas and new schemes. When it came to soul or disco music, areas where historically EMI had failed miserably over the years, our cunning plan was to launch our own disco label under the rather hip name Sidewalk. Our hope was that nobody would realise that this new label, with its striking yellow and black logo (I think it was red and black on LPs), and American-ised name, came out of Manchester Square, home to Cliff, Kate, Floyd and Queen. While we might not have fooled all of the people all of the time, we did manage to get a handful of hits for the likes of Gonzalez and David Bendeth but Sidewalk was an experiment that lasted for just one year.

Chapter 8

ANARCHY AT EMI

Before I even met the Sex Pistols, I voiced my concerns to my boss Bob Mercer when he told me that we were hoping to sign the band. I told him I didn't get what they were about and couldn't see any real benefits in doing a deal despite some parts of the media getting on their bandwagon. Mercer, a sometimes blunt Northerner, soon put me straight, explaining "This is all about kids who are unemployed, are unemployable, and have no chance of doing anything. It's got nothing to do with you as a near 30-year-old professional with a career." That said, he then added, "It's exciting and if we can get them it will be great for all of us."

And get them we did, thanks to the efforts of A&R head Nick Mobbs who saw off opposition from Chrysalis and Polydor to sign the Pistols to a two year, two album deal for an advance of £40,000. They, like a few other EMI acts over the years, spent some time in the small studio on the ground floor at Manchester Square, which doubled as a presentation room on occasions, working on the first single 'Anarchy In The UK'.

However, when people around the company - certainly

promotion people and sales reps - heard the song they were quick to voice their disapproval and concerns, suggesting the band couldn't play and that getting it into shops and on the radio was going to be a problem. It's a fact that EMI held a particular fascination for the Pistols' manager Malcolm McLaren. We were big and corporate and he relished the idea of his band of scallywags being part of the establishment and of having their records released on the EMI label. Yet, they were assigned to the Harvest division of the company as it was thought that it was used to dealing with 'oddballs' and left-field musicians.

As I'd been told by Bob Mercer that me and the Pistols were probably poles apart musically and in most other ways, I assigned my colleague Tom Nolan to look after the band - and he was delighted to be working with the latest sensation. The Pistols were infrequent visitors to Manchester Square although McLaren seemed to pop in and set up camp in any spare office he could find and use it as his business headquarters.

Despite the band's rare appearances, there were some memorable moments when they did show up. We discovered that Johnny Rotten wasn't keen on being called 'John' - so obviously that's what we called him at every opportunity just to piss him off. He got his own back when, during press interviews organised by Tom Nolan, he'd go into an office with a journalist and ensure that the door was locked and the key removed so nobody could leave, or get in, until he was ready.

He was also a dab hand with a marker pen and spent odd moments in my press office scrawling designs and pictures on scraps of paper. The walls lining the stairs from reception to the first floor of Manchester Square were adorned with photos of the great and good of EMI over the years and

Rotten made his mark on some of them – drawing glasses on Olivia Newton-John and a moustache on opera singer Maria Callas.

Thinking back, maybe we should have collected up John's efforts with a view to selling them later as early works from the Rotten period. I remember Abbey Road Studios boss Ken Townsend telling me that if people had known how famous The Beatles would become, they would have kept every knife, fork and tea cup the foursome had ever touched.

I was happy to sit in the background and let Tom Nolan deal with the press enquiries involving the Pistols and their manager as their debut single 'Anarchy In The UK' was readied for release on November 26, 1976. Because of delays in recording, the record was delayed and lost its dubious claim to be first punk single when The Damned put out 'New Rose' a month earlier.

However, things took a giant turn for the worse when promotion chief Eric Hall got them on the Thames TV show *Today* hosted by Bill Grundy on December 1. They were set to replace Queen who, depending which story you believe, had to pull out because their video for 'Somebody To Love' hadn't been cleared for broadcast by the Musician's Union OR because Freddie Mercury was still recovering from some serious dental work.

Either way, Queen were off and Hall was left with the problem of keeping the show's producer Mike Housego happy by finding a replacement but in fact, it was Housego who asked about the Sex Pistols appearing. Hall sold the idea to McLaren, who was hoping for a major nationwide TV show, but only by agreeing to the manager's very un-punk requests for a limo, complete with smoked salmon and champagne, to take the band to the studio. Aware that pitching the Sex Pistols with veteran (and renowned grumpy) interviewer Grundy might not go entirely smoothly, Hall warned Thames TV to be careful.

As it turned out, it didn't go well at all. The Pistols were joined in the studio by Siouxsie Sioux and Steve Severin from the Banshees plus some hangers-on from something called the Bromley Contingent. There was a belief that both the band and the show's host had drunk a little too much and pretty soon it kicked off live on-air when Grundy asked them to "say something outrageous." Steve Jones responded by calling Grundy a "dirty bastard" and a "f***king rotter." And all this was being broadcast at 6.25pm as families in the London area sat down for their tea.

There was an immediate response with Thames TV broadcasting numerous apologies during the evening and those of us at EMI who missed the actual broadcast for various reasons - and that included EMI Records managing director Leslie Hill, my boss Mercer, Hall and myself - soon became aware of what had gone on.

The following day's papers were full of it with the *Daily Mirror's* headline reading "The Filth And The Fury" and the *Daily Mail* running with "Four-Letter Punk Group In TV Storm." There was even a story of a lorry driver kicking in his television screen in protest at the language he and his young son had been exposed to. The phones in my office rang non-stop as the story grew and grew, but we were all under strict instructions to say nothing while people much higher up the ladder analysed what had gone on and decided on the best course of action.

As soon as he remembered that EMI actually owned 50% of Thames TV, Bob Mercer decided to call the station's Controller Jeremy Isaacs to get his reaction and he was relieved to hear Isaacs say that he had suspended Grundy, explaining, "Your boys used some very bad language but they were provoked." Happy that they didn't have to grovel or apologise for EMI Records or the Pistols, Mercer and Hill still had to contend with the powers-that-be within the EMI corporation.

While I was getting calls from the weekly music papers who could wait a few days for an up-date, the dailies were less patient and my equivalent within EMI Limited, Bryan Samain, was left to issue a statement which said, "Anything that does not enhance the behaviour or conduct of the company is disgraceful. We shall be looking into it."

In addition to the media, there was a storm brewing within the financial community in the City of London and outrage from shareholders and some staff from other divisions of the company. While the press were lapping up the story, radio stations were less impressed and slowly but surely the record disappeared from playlists up and down the country. BBC Radio One decided that it was unsuitable for day-time radio while Capital Radio in London and stations in Birmingham, Sheffield and Manchester dropped the single.

The strange part about it was that they were making the decision based on the group's behaviour on the Thames TV show rather than the record's content which was not overly offensive. But, despite all this activity, we calculated that around 9,000 records had been sold in the first week of release. This was despite the ladies working in the EMI factory refusing to pack the record in protest at the bad language, which brought a response from EMI corporate saying that while the company didn't condone the use of bad language, "there was no question of any action being taken against the Sex Pistols."

I had no involvement in any of the statements coming

from 'upstairs' and didn't know whether Hill or Mercer, or McLaren for that matter, were ever consulted but it was clear that McLaren was happy to milk the situation, simply suggesting that "boys will be boys" while enjoying all the attention his band and their record were receiving.

EMI's sister company in America, Capitol Records, took a stronger line and basically banned all punk records and groups that they branded as "profane" and then, as the Pistols set about their first UK tour, things arguably went from bad to worse.

Before the fall-out from the Grundy incident, the band were booked for 19 shows from Norwich to Glasgow and Plymouth to Dundee but that was soon whittled down to three - Leeds, Manchester and Plymouth. Some replacement dates were added but it was all falling apart around everybody's ears. When it came round to EMI's annual general meeting just a week after the *Today* show, EMI chairman Sir John Read explained that the issue of releasing further records from the Pistols "will have to be carefully considered" and confirmed that EMI would "do everything we can to restrain their public behaviour."

While the tour limped on around the country, and the band members were accused of spitting, swearing and trashing hotels, complaints continued to be aired by politicians, shareholders, EMI executive directors and from somewhere called Radar and Equipment Accounts, which I think, was part of the company's Defence Systems Division. A total of 26 employees signed a letter written to EMI's in-house newspaper following the Pistols' appearance on the *Today* programme saying, "As employees of EMI we must protest strongly that this organisation should be associated with this group whose speech and behaviour is offensive in the extreme."

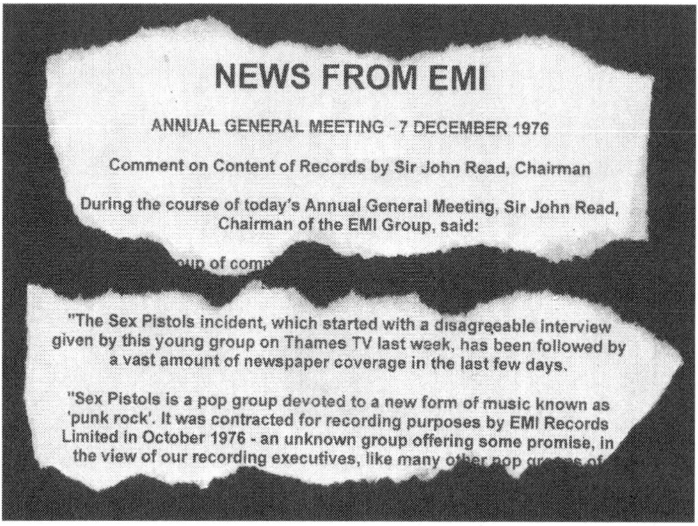
NEWS FROM EMI

ANNUAL GENERAL MEETING - 7 DECEMBER 1976

Comment on Content of Records by Sir John Read, Chairman

During the course of today's Annual General Meeting, Sir John Read, Chairman of the EMI Group, said:

"The Sex Pistols incident, which started with a disagreeable interview given by this young group on Thames TV last week, has been followed by a vast amount of newspaper coverage in the last few days.

"Sex Pistols is a pop group devoted to a new form of music known as 'punk rock'. It was contracted for recording purposes by EMI Records Limited in October 1976 - an unknown group offering some promise, in the view of our recording executives, like many

The corporate view of the Pistols, from EMI's AGM in 1976

Our response was to write back to these Defence people who, we were always told, only made systems for defence and not attack (which none of us actually believed) stating our disgust at what they did and dis-associating ourselves from them. It was a bit petty but it was as far as we got in dealing with the backlash, as a new memo went out to all Records' people reminding them that I was the only point of contact and every request and question was to be shovelled round to me so that I could send it 'upstairs' to corporate. In my view I was sort of in the picture but still outside looking in.

While all this was going on, the single 'Anarchy In The UK' was racing up the UK chart and, after four weeks in the shops (only some of them) and with very limited radio play, it reached a high point of No. 38 in the singles listing in a month when Chicago's 'If You Leave Me Now',

Showaddywaddy's 'Under The Moon Of Love' and 'When A Child Is Born' by Johnny Mathis all topped the chart.

Malcolm McLaren was still adding fuel to the fire and told the major music papers that he was "thoroughly disgusted with the attitude of people involved in the British music scene who wanted to suppress this new wave of punk bands" and then he turned his attention to EMI saying, "EMI say they are behind us but as far as I can see they seem to be miles behind us." This, at least, forced EMI's corporate folk to confirm that the company's "whole attitude needs rethinking and we are still considering the Sex Pistols contract."

One division of EMI Records was however still trying to do their best by the group and their record and our International Department booked the band on a Dutch TV show called *Disco Circus*, but the trip by plane from Heathrow to Holland on January 4 brought another shit storm. That evening's *Evening News* carried - under the banner headline "These Revolting VIPS! Sex Pistols in Rumpus At Airport" - a report that the band had "caused uproar" and suggested that they "vomited and spat" on their way to the plane. This obviously caused another panic at EMI headquarters as the next day's press carried the same stories.

This prompted Read to call a well-placed contact he had in the airline business to ask if it was all true. And, it seems, he was assured that it all happened just as the papers said.

EMI's man on the trip with the band was International exec Graham Fletcher and he was convinced nothing untoward had happened and told that to both Hill and Mercer as they prepared for another inquisition with Chairman Read.

When Mercer was told by the company's chairman that

he was convinced the reports were true, he tried explaining that the 'contact' wasn't actually there and might be exaggerating things or simply going along with the press reports but his protestations fell on stony ground.

Read's argument was that it didn't really matter whether or not the incident at Heathrow took place as outside perception was now more important than the facts and he was particularly concerned with how government officials, shareholders and investors might view things. It was becoming clear to all of us - and Hill and Mercer in particular - that the end was in sight.

Despite arguments about the negative effect on company morale and the record division's ability to sign further acts, Read was adamant that it was all over. Hill flew to Holland to break the news to McLaren that the band were being sacked by EMI and a press release was typed up and released from EMI's Group Press Relations office, dated January 6. It read: "EMI and the Sex Pistols group have mutually agreed to terminate their recording contract. EMI feels unable to promote this group's records internationally in view of the adverse publicity which has been generated over the last two months, although recent press reports of the behaviour of the Sex Pistols appear to have been exaggerated."

So maybe Read did finally accept that his contact wasn't quite as reliable as he thought. The release ended with an assurance to all in the record business that, "The termination of this contract with the Sex Pistols does not in any way affect EMI's intention to remain active in all areas of the music business."

In the light of the sacking of the Pistols, Mercer called all of us who worked for him to a meeting and said that he recognised that we all had the choice of resigning on principle or staying but, he admitted, "Nothing is going to change what is happening."

One man who was not reassured was A&R chief Mobbs who had actually signed the Pistols and championed their cause within the company.

He was intent on resigning in protest but when Mercer refused to accept it, he agreed to stay although the word went out that he was open to offers.

The rest of us chatted among ourselves as to the best course of action. EMI Limited would not be moved by a mass walkout despite the bad press it might generate. They wouldn't be held to ransom by a bunch of long-haired louts but simply replace us all or even sell the music division.

Both Hill and Mercer made clear to me their disappointment at the decision made by our corporate masters but on January 17 a statement was issued from Hill which stated, "In accordance with the previously stated wishes of both parties and the verbal telephone agreement made on Tuesday 6 January, the documents terminating the contract between EMI and the Sex Pistols have now been signed. EMI Records wish the Sex Pistols every success with their next recording contract."

Those documents confirmed that the Sex Pistols and McLaren would receive the £20,000 balance from their record deal advance plus a further £10,000 from the termination of their deal with EMI Music Publishing. And ironically, despite our best wishes for "their next recording contract", it only lasted six days as A&M Records fired the Pistols and this time they managed to gather a further £75,000 for less than a week's work.

They then went on to sign with Virgin and had a much more successful relationship which included seven Top 10 singles and a No.1 album. But still things rumbled on with the Pistols and EMI and Read's argument about perception being all-important was sort of proved right when a letter arrived in June 1977 addressed to EMI Chairman Sir Joseph Lockwood.

It came from Neville Trotter, Tory MP for Tynemouth, on House of Commons headed notepaper, and he wrote to complain about the single 'God Save The Queen', saying, "I was very surprised to hear that your company are producing the above record which refers in a most offensive way to H.M The Queen. It seems singularly inappropriate that you should have contributed to the Jubilee in this way." He went on to add, "While you may feel it justifiable to earn money producing 'punk' records, I would have thought that you could have made an exception in this case."

Unfortunately, Mr. Trotter had somehow got it all wrong and failed to realise that Lockwood had retired in 1974 and that 'God Save The Queen' was released by Virgin Records some four months after we had sacked the band.

Even after all the media hullabaloo about the Pistols' behaviour, their music and very public sacking from EMI, it was slightly odd to realise that everything associated with them came back to haunt EMI. After all, we only had them for 90 days and released just one (minor hit) record but being involved in what has gone down as a genuine part of Britain's music history was a memorable and unique experience.

On the back of those 90 days, I catalogued all the events in the book *Sex Pistols 90 Days At EMI* which came out in 2007. And Sex Pistol Glen Matlock was kind enough to write the Introduction in which he said quite candidly, "I don't think I blame EMI for what happened. I know that if none of that happened at EMI then the whole Sex Pistols myth and mystique wouldn't have been what it was."

NEVILLE TROTTER, F.C.A., J.P., M.P.

HOUSE OF COMMONS
LONDON SW1A OAA

24th June, 1977

Sir Joseph Lockwood,
Chairman,
E.M.I. Records,
E.M.I. House,
Manchester Square,
London
W1A 1ES

Dear Sir Joseph

<u>Record : "God Save The Queen"</u>

I was very surprised to hear that your Company are producing the above record which refers in a most offensive way to H.M. The Queen. It seems singularly inappropriate that you should have contributed to the Jubilee in this way.

While you may feel it justifiable to earn money producing 'punk' records, I would have thought that you could have made an exception in this case. Might I suggest that no further copies of this record are issued. Its production has certainly lowered my estimation of your Company and many members of the public share my views.

I would welcome your comments.

Yours sincerely

Neville Trotter

Whoops! An MP blames EMI for something they didn't do with the Pistols

I was flattered to get a positive three star review in the esteemed music magazine *Q* when the reviewer wrote, "With plenty of eye-of-the-storm detail and commentary, it tells the story with a refreshing absence of myth-making. Even seasoned Pistols bores will come away with a better idea of one of punk's key moments of sticking it to the establishment."

At the same time *Record Collector* offered another three star assessment, saying, "Southall's blow by blow account from inside the EMI press office is fascinating stuff."

And, incidentally, when I go and talk to students in colleges and universities around the country - and despite the fact that I worked with the solo Beatles, Pink Floyd, Queen, Kate Bush and the Rolling Stones amongst others - it's the Sex Pistols that generate most interest. And I never wonder why!

In the wake of the Pistols debacle, and while there was no official word from on high to say so, we all knew that any new signings we made would probably catch the eye of the main EMI Board – who would be monitoring things closely in case Records screwed up again!

In fact Bob Mercer was all for trying to embarrass the EMI directors by asking for their approval about every act and even song lyrics.

Leslie Hill, on the other hand, decided that the less Corporate knew the better.

He certainly wasn't going to let them know about a Pink Floyd song from the album *Animals* with four "f***s" in it and a less than complimentary reference to morality campaigner Mary Whitehouse. He reckoned that if the board members didn't know about it or read about it, then it was best left alone.

Had they been aware, who knows what they would have

said in light of the album reaching No.1 and passing the one million sales mark in the UK.

There was, obviously, more concern when it came to signing any punk acts, but Mercer relished going to Read to tell him about one of our new signings. Mercer told me that when he mentioned to Read that we had signed a new punk band, the Chairman just said "jolly good" and when he was told that the Tom Robinson Band had a gay lead singer, he just said "jolly good" again.

That was one hurdle over and despite our concerns about acts post the Pistols debacle shying away from EMI, we did add Australian punk act The Saints, plus Wire and the Gang Of Four to the roster without any hiccups. And in one final twist we welcomed original Sex Pistol Glen Matlock (he left the band just after their firing by EMI to be replaced by Sid Vicious) back into the fold with his new band, The Rich Kids. As Nick Mobbs explained, Matlock was "fine with the A&R, marketing and promo people ... we had to make sure he had no contact with corporate EMI."

The signing of Tom Robinson and his 'gay punk' band came after a particularly raucous night in a Camden pub when they played a mighty fine set in front of an audience featuring many an A&R (artists and repertoire) person from a host of record companies.

Bob Mercer was at the heart of it and, after negotiations that began that night and ended the next day, we bagged TRB. Being in the middle of a crowd of people - including many manly men - singing along to 'Glad To Be Gay' was a uniquely joyous experience.

Chapter 9

QUEEN RULE OK

Months before the Sex Pistols loomed large in all our lives, I became more involved with Queen, the four young men who had pilfered albums from my office at Tamla Motown a couple of years earlier. In that time Freddie Mercury, Brian May, Roger Taylor and John Deacon had notched up five hit singles - including the record-breaking 'Bohemian Rhapsody' - and their first number one album with *A Night At The Opera*. And sadly, I can't claim credit for any of them as I wasn't involved.

However, when they switched management from Trident to John Reid, the manager of Elton John, in the autumn of 1975 I found myself in Reid's offices arranging a contract-signing photo session. I presume I was the band's stand-in press officer as Tony Brainsby, their PR for three years (and the main PR man for most rock stars back then), came - and went - with their Trident deal. They would eventually get independent representation but I got the gig for a few weeks.

A year later I found myself at a playback for the band's album *A Day At The Races* and as impressive as it was – it would be their second No.1 album – I wasn't destined to work on it as I think by then the band had appointed Phil Symes as their press agent.

Then things took a turn to my benefit early in 1977, after we had sacked the Sex Pistols and life was getting back to a rock'n'roll normal.

Queen were about to head off to America for a major tour and Symes had lined up three important journalists to cover the initial dates and interview the band. They were Bob Hart from the *Sun*, Harry Doherty from *Melody Maker* and Mick Brown, the London writer for *Rolling Stone*. The plan was for Symes to accompany them to New York for the shows at Madison Square Garden and in New Jersey ... and seemingly for EMI to pay all the expenses for both the writers and Symes. Anyone who knew EMI back then, even though the regime was becoming a lot looser and more reasonable, knew this was NOT going to happen and sure enough Symes was sidelined and I got a ticket to make my debut visit to the USA. And not only was I going with three journalists I knew and liked, I discovered that the support band on the tour were Thin Lizzy, which meant I would be there with good friend Philip Lynott. Things were going from good to great.

The flights to America for all four of us were booked by EMI's travel department which was always on the lookout for a bargain and we found ourselves joining an Air India flight from the sub-continent as it stopped in London on its way to New York. It was crowded and noisy and memorably one disgruntled Indian passenger actually told a stewardess that the trouble with the service was because "There are too many Chiefs and not enough Indians." Looking at a passenger load in excess of 250, he was probably technically correct but I didn't much care as I was wrapped up in the excitement of making my first transatlantic flight.

However, when we landed in the US, Bob Hart, a much-travelled Australian who had experienced the best and worst that US Immigration could throw at you, offered a few words of advice - “run for it!”

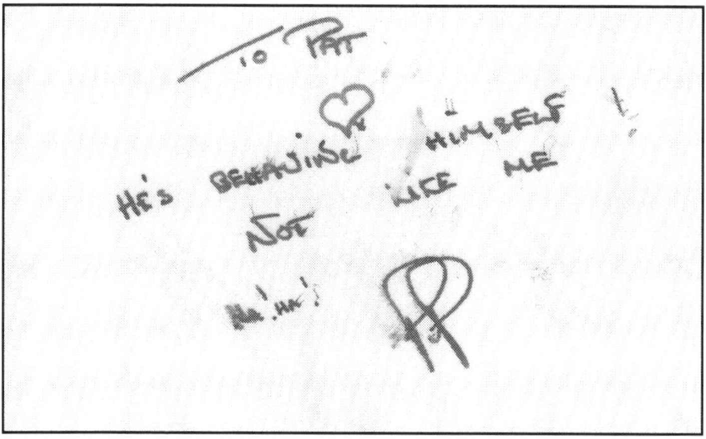

Philip Lynott (left - so he says) and Thin Lizzy band mates Brian Robertson, Scott Gorham and Brian Downey. The picture postcard home includes Philip’s brief but reassuring note to my wife

Bob's plan was to make a fast dash for the Immigration booths before the passengers from India and beyond started arriving and experiencing all the baggage that America's finest border control officers could throw at them. We made it to Immigration where we were stopped in our tracks by an official who asked "Why the hurry?" When we explained that there were a lot of passengers from India and elsewhere behind us, he stamped us through, drew down the blind on his booth saying 'closed' and went off for an early dinner or late lunch. Either way, I was in the land of the free but even then I wasn't quite ready for the cab ride into Manhattan as the famous skyline I'd only seen in movies and on TV shows came into view. The whole ride into the city was through snow covered streets with a couple of feet of the stuff swept up on the sidewalks (I'd already got the lingo) and then the Chrysler and Empire State buildings came into view plus the Brooklyn Bridge and the twin towers of the World Trade Centre - God, it was glorious and mind-blowing!

Equally exciting, was checking into the Plaza Hotel next to Central Park with its palm court orchestra, fancy tea room and assorted bars including the exotic Trader Vic's. And there was a bit of star spotting to be done as Paul Simon was darting about the place trying not to be noticed and I even shared a lift with Charlie Chaplin and a lady I presumed to be his wife plus some kids and maybe grandchildren.

We must have arrived a day before the Queen show as I took a walk around the next day with Mick Brown who, as a veteran of the city, made sure we visited a snow-bound Jones Street in the West Village where Bob Dylan and his girlfriend had been photographed in the snow for the cover of *The Freewheelin' Bob Dylan* album.

Going to Madison Square Garden for the first time was equally exciting and having deposited three journos in their seats, I went backstage to see the band where Brian May was taking photos of everything in sight with his new Polaroid instant camera. I wandered off to find a toilet and on the way ran into a large janitor who gave me directions but then took me aside to show me a side room. Then, in hushed tones, he said, "This is where Muhammed Ali changed when he fought Joe Frazier." I wasn't sure what I was looking at other than a large white tiled room but I was happy to use the toilet - which was maybe where Ali ...

Playing to a sold out Garden, Queen debuted 'Somebody To Love' on this tour and also played full length versions of both 'Bohemian Rhapsody' and 'Brighton Rock', and then we all retired to a party somewhere in New York where the rich, famous and even infamous of the city assembled and Freddie Mercury went into full prima donna mode.

I caught up with Philip Lynott the next day and we went out, not quite on the town, but around and about in a freezing New York City. He warned me about the wind-chill factor which was at about -25° and the perils of breathing in when your mouth was not covered. Somewhere along the way - as Lynott was keen to cause a bit of a stir - we went into an Irish bar where a six-foot-plus black man with a huge Afro was bound to 'cause a stir'. It was only when he spoke to order a Guinness in a thick Dublin accent that the locals eased back in their seats, with some of them even recognizing the rock star son of a mother from Dublin and a father from what was British Guiana.

The following night's concert was in New Jersey and it was there before the show that Queen gave a couple of interviews. I think Bob Hart and Harry Doherty left the next day while I had lunch with the band in the Waldorf

Hotel where they were staying. It was my first taste of Japanese food - very nice - and meant I spent some time with Brian May, John Deacon and Roger Taylor (Freddie was off somewhere else) which was also very nice. While May had his new camera, Deacon, the electronics wiz, had a fancy new watch on which he could calculate all sorts of things including the band's royalties!

January 8 and it was off to Syracuse in upstate New York by plane, despite the treacherous conditions underfoot and possibly in the air. Mick Brown was travelling on the plane where he would get his chance to talk to the band but first there were seats to be confirmed. I'm not sure what sort of plane it was but it wasn't a fancy big jet although it did have a smart class upfront and a not so smart class at the back. We were booked into the back bit while the band, obviously, had the whole of the front part.

My job was to get myself and Mick Brown upgraded to the front but the conversation with the American lady travel agent didn't go that well. She said there was only one seat left in business or whatever it was called, so I told her to give it to Brown and I would travel economy. She then said OK to that and confirmed I would be travelling 'coach'. I said I wasn't going to go on a bus but had to be on the plane with everybody else. She then repeated that I was booked 'coach' and again I protested that I couldn't in all honesty travel by bus from New York to Syracuse and get there in time.

Then it all dropped into place as she explained that 'coach' was economy in America plane seat lingo and she confirmed that I was on the plane with everybody else. Economy/coach, pavement/sidewalk, jam/jelly, bumper/fender, lavatory/john, petrol/gas ... it was all becoming clear that we didn't actually speak the same language.

Landing in Syracuse - which was about 250 miles from New York and birthplace of both Richard Gere and Tom Cruise - was fraught with danger as the only things visible in the airport car park were the tops of car radio aerials, everything else was covered in about three feet of snow. The show was at the War Memorial Auditorium which was home to the local ice hockey team, Syracuse Crunch. Which explained why it was so damn cold in there.

After the show it was back to what was presumably the best hotel in town and a late night trip to the top floor - of about seven - for a drink, linking up with Brian May, his then wife Chrissie, and some others. We were all entertained by a singer who was once a member of the fifties hit vocal group the Platters, and I wondered whether one ex-Platter should be called a plate!

From Syracuse it was on to Boston for my last date on Queen's *A Day At The Races* tour and it was here that for some reason that I still don't understand, I fell out with Queen's tour manager Pete Brown. In the lobby of the hotel - looking over a very frozen Charles River complete with ice skaters - he told me that I had let the band down and not shown them the respect they deserved. I had no idea then, or now for that matter, what he was on about but he was obviously upset about something. Whatever it was, it hadn't upset Brian May as he told me everything was OK, the band were fine and I was still persona grata. I called Bob Mercer at EMI in London to tell him that if Brown called to complain, I had no idea what he was on about and that as far as I knew the band were fine with everything - including me. Seemingly Brown never called my boss and I never had the chance to ask what had upset him in America as he left Queen a year or so later and sadly died in 1993. The mystery lives on.

Leaving the Queen tour in Boston, I made my way to California to meet up with the people at Capitol Records, EMI's company in Los Angeles, and found myself driving around LA in the hire car supplied by Capitol - a Ford Pinto which was the smallest car in Ford's US range and described as 'sub-compact'. I think I was the only person staying at the luxurious 5 star Beverly Wilshire Hotel (as featured in the film *Oh Pretty Woman*) driving such a crap car, but I managed to find my way to the world famous Capitol Tower, the offices built in 1956 to resemble a stack of records.

I hung out with the people there for a few days, did some shopping and sightseeing and went to the movies (or pictures) to see the 1976 remake of *King Kong* starring Jeff Bridges and Jessica Lange. It was showing in a small cinema on Wilshire Boulevard and at the finish I strolled back to the Wilshire Hotel. It was dark and I was smoking a fine cigar (not Cuban obviously) when a police car pulled up alongside me and a cop got out - no guns were on show – and asked me what I was doing. In my finest British accent I told him I had been to the pictures and was now on my way back to my hotel – the Beverly Wilshire. He looked me up and down – all shoulder length hair, beard and flared jeans (me not him) and – despite the good-sized cigar – told me, "Ain't no shit like you stays at the Beverly Wilshire." I assured him that I was a guest at the fine hotel but didn't have my room key about my person.

They let me go but kerb-crawled me all the way along the boulevard and watched me go into the hotel, when - in a friendly Anglo-American gesture – I gave them a good-bye wave.

Without picking out the exact towns and cities where I saw Queen perform over the years – and there were a few

- I always had this vision of what went on when Brian May got his moment in the spotlight to perform 'Brighton Rock'. On the album, the guitar solo lasted about three minutes but live on stage, he was allowed anything up to around 13 minutes to astound and amaze us with his guitar wizardry. But what, I always wondered, did the other three do with their time backstage? I had visions of John Deacon fiddling with the latest electronic gadget while Roger Taylor maybe had a takeaway delivered and Freddie Mercury ... well, who knew what the flamboyant singer might get up to!

Back in England, where I had moved over into EMI's marketing division, it was becoming clear that Queen were not like the other bands we had signed. They turned up for marketing meetings, discussed album artwork and potential giveaways for the media, although not all of them went down that well. One 'gift'- not half as popular as the clocks - was a sweat shirt emblazoned with the word 'Queen' and it soon became apparent that they weren't for everybody.

We never knew whether this was a joke by the band to see who would (and wouldn't) wear them, but all of us at EMI wore them whenever there was a possibility a band member might drop in.

Actually, Freddie did drop in one day for lunch with me and my marketing pal Ian Groves and we went off to a fancy French restaurant on a corner of Manchester Square. Despite the fine cuisine, Mercury was content with a salad - and a small one at that - while we tucked into all sorts of expensive stuff, but then again we were paying. After lunch, as we emerged into the sunshine, Mercury decided he would walk with us around the two sides of the square back to the office. As we made our way, walking the fifty or so yards back to EMI, I noticed that Mercury's limo was cruising at walking pace alongside us. I asked the singer what that was all about and he said, "You never know my darling, I might get recognised and have to jump in quickly." If I ever needed convincing that Mercury was a star, and not ashamed or embarrassed to be one, that was the moment.

It's not unusual for an artist already signed to a record company to bring along other acts that they rated, or were friends with. Freddie Mercury was no exception. He offered us the chance in 1977 to work with Peter Straker who was signed to his newly formed Goose Productions. Straker was a Jamaican-born singer and actor who had appeared in the original production of *Hair!* and he was a friend of Mercury, who invested around £20,000 of his own hard-earned cash into Straker's debut album *This One's On Me*. It wasn't a great album despite being co-produced by Mercury and Queen's producer Roy Thomas Baker, but it perfectly illustrated the lengths record companies would occasionally go to keep a major star happy.

At that time, I was working in Artist Development, a division which was an adjunct to A&R where three of us helped up and coming acts to find managers, agents, producers (records and videos) and designers. John Preston, John Bagnall and I worked on the likes of Gryphon, Kate Bush and Peter Straker - plus some others I can't remember - and I was handed Straker which meant long conversations with Mercury about image, promotion and a UK tour. However, they often ended up as chats about *Coronation Street*, one of Freddie Mercury's favourite TV shows, or Japanese furniture, another of Mercury's favourites. The tour did go ahead and I went out on the road (with my wife for company) and we flew to Edinburgh for the opening night and popped along again when Straker was in Birmingham to play, I think, the local Odeon which, on a good day held over 2,400 people. The Beatles had played there as had the Rolling Stones and Queen when it was no doubt packed to the rafters, but sadly for Straker that was not the case.

I think we were looking at less than a hundred tickets sold and despite our best efforts to get Straker to go down with a cold or throat infection and call the whole thing off, he was adamant that "the show must go on my dears." And sure enough, he went out and did his set dressed in tight satin pants, high heels and a feather boa and his only concession to the poor crowd, who had all been moved into the front stalls, was when it came to the song 'That Old Black Magic'. He usually wandered into the audience with a huge box of Black Magic and made jokes about "nut clusters" and "hard centres" but, with tongue firmly in cheek, he went out this night with just a bag of Revels.

I last saw him in 1979 in The Who's *Tommy* when I went along to the London theatre with his manager and her husband, who was something in the City. He came along a little late, wearing a huge sort of poacher's coat from which he produced a bottle of champagne and three glasses – and we toasted Straker's performance as the Narrator.

May 1984 was the last time I spent any time with Queen and Freddie Mercury in particular. During the Montreux Pop Festival in Switzerland we all assembled on a boat on Lake Geneva for a reception hosted (but probably not paid for) by the band.

I was there with an editor from *Billboard*, a strapping blond, six foot, good looking all-American man who immediately caught Freddie's eye.

The singer said to me "oh he's nice, who is he, do you know him?" I said he was a friend of mine from America and when Freddie asked if he might be gay I, to my shame, didn't disillusion him.

At that point Freddie set out after him, following him around the boat trying to catch his eye. The American's only escape was to lock himself in a toilet and stay there until we disembarked when I owned up to what I had done. Despite me buying him copious amounts of champagne, it took him a good few weeks to forgive me. And funnily enough he turned down an invitation for a few of us to join Freddie in his suite overlooking the lake for late night drinks. I went, of course, safe in the knowledge that Freddie didn't fancy me one little bit.

Chapter 10

IT'S EMI'S PARTY

Sales conferences were an almost essential annual event in a record company's autumn calendar. They brought together the company's sales force, its executives and marketing teams in a once a year jamboree of presentations, shows, dinners and an amount of bad behaviour.

The first one I attended was in around 1977 at a fancy hotel in Eastbourne where we, EMI's UK division, were presenting product (that was the very business-like term we used for records) by Queen, Cliff Richard and I think Cilla Black's last EMI album after her 15 year stint with the company. She was in fact performing twice nightly in Eastbourne while we were there and she made some tickets available for people to go along to her show. My colleagues and I couldn't go as we were rehearsing with slides, projectors and speeches but Cilla decided to pop along and surprise us after her show while we were in mid-rehearsal. Her husband Bobby was with her and maybe he'd had a drink or was just naturally bolshie but, when whoever was on stage and blinded by a spotlight, was interrupted by the unannounced guests and shouted "what the f***'s going on?", Willis immediately challenged them to a fight

- in broad Scouse. "Come down here and say that and I'll sort you out," he yelled. Thankfully Cilla stepped in and quickly placated her old man who went away mumbling and grumbling to himself.

Our other near embarrassing moment came thanks to one of the company's longest serving marketing managers, Colin Burn. He was a bit of a cynic about most things and often, and quite deliberately, came out with the wrong (but usually funny) lines at the wrong time. One of his favourites was a put down about something that the rest of us found amusing or enjoyable with the line, "I've not had so much fun since I cleaned my shoes this morning."

He once told executives from the American ABC Dunhill label – who had signed the Four Tops and brought them to the UK to tour and promote their album released through EMI - that had the quartet of musicians been any later for the reception in their honour, "We would have had the first topless party in EMI's history." They didn't laugh.

Our concern was Burn finding some way to cock-up our carefully prepared and rehearsed presentations and our worst nightmare came true as we had a final run-through of our slides in an ante room at the hotel. In a generous gesture, Burn offered to stand guard over things while we went to get a quick bite to eat. When we returned we thought we would have one final run through and sure enough we discovered why Burn had been so helpful. Our presentation was now littered with a quite bizarre selection of obscene slides which were too graphic to describe even now but rest assured they would NOT have helped Cilla's farewell *Modern Priscilla* album and might even have set off another round of fisticuffs with her old man.

Conferences were held at hotels at Heathrow Airport and in towns and cities around the country including

Bournemouth, Newcastle, Blackpool, Torquay and, the less glamourous, Holiday Inn Slough. In the later years, organising a conference usually involved the personnel (or human resources) department working with me in PR, although I never quite worked out why. Maybe it was to try and answer a question nobody could answer - who is gay and who do they share a room with?

There were at least two openly homosexual guys within the EMI Records set up - there were maybe a few more who remained in the closet - but when it came to allocating conference rooms it gave personnel a headache. Below a certain executive level, delegates shared rooms at these shindigs and the easy way out was to put the gay guys together even if they didn't like each other. Alternatively, asking a non-homosexual to share with a homosexual was asking for more trouble than personnel knew how to handle. The compromise was to make the gay guys a 'special' case and give them a room on their own even though their straight counterparts still had to share which brought another round of complaints.

Another issue that was apparent throughout my time in EMI Records was that there were very few women in senior positions - indeed the history of EMI wasn't littered with female executives. There were ladies who were marketing and production managers, press officers and promotion staff, but all the top dogs were men and we were all white. During the early eighties somebody from some media organisation decided to investigate the British record industry to show that it was racist. They weren't looking to see if it was, having already decided that it was, but needed some evidence to prove their point. In all honesty, I don't know whether it was deliberately racist – it certainly wasn't a policy I ever encountered – but the fact remained that there were very few black people in the record business. I was asked by these people if I had ever hired a black person and, if not, why not? The only answer I could give was that I had never interviewed a black person for any job at EMI and had no idea whether there had ever been any black applicants. Back then, the list of people applying for a role would be vetted by the personnel department and they would then send through a list of potential candidates.

Now whether the buck should have stopped with personnel I don't know. Did they get loads of applications from would-be black press officers and marketing managers or accountants and lawyers? It was certainly a time - in the 1970s and 1980s - when there were very few black managers or promoters or producers or lawyers in the music business but I don't know whose fault that was - or if it was anybody's fault. In 1986 I actually appointed the first woman to a job in EMI Records with the title Director - and she was Asian. Just to be clear I didn't give her the job because she was female or because of her colour - she was just bloody good!

We often invited acts to perform at conferences and one of these was Roy Harper. Roy bizarrely chose to offer up some political messages in his set to a room full of less than interested (or sober) sales folk before being followed at the top of the bill by the much more cheery and up-beat Hot Chocolate.

At the Heathrow Hotel in 1977, we went for a sporting theme and hired ace sports presenter Dickie Davies to act as the host throughout our Saturday afternoon programme. As it was probably late August or early September he, of course, was actually in a TV studio somewhere doing his proper job presenting ITV's *World of Sport*. We recorded him a week or so earlier and got him to run through our new releases and, while we had to bring him up to date with some of the names, it would be hard to find a more professional and charming man. He ran through it all in very few takes and on the Saturday afternoon, in the hotel conference theatre, we gave out football scarves and rattles and pre-paid pools coupons as we cut to Davies for the live broadcast of the football scores. And to top it off, Brian May and Roger Taylor from Queen brought down a preview copy of their next single which we played as the conference finale. Hearing 'We Are The Champions' belting out of the speakers for the first time was a wonderful moment and guaranteed that it was not going to be just a chart hit but a sporting anthem.

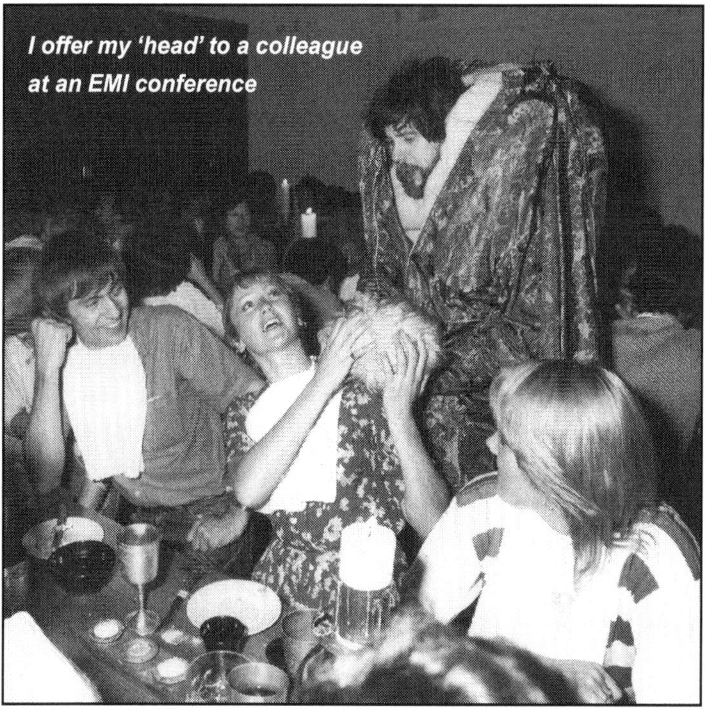

I offer my 'head' to a colleague at an EMI conference

To begin with, we weren't short of creative themes for our conferences. The Newcastle event involved an Elizabethan dinner at the supposedly haunted Lumley Castle where some of us decided to dress up accordingly (I was the headless man). While the 1980 Slough extravaganza (by now money was getting tight) included a set by Don McLean who had reached number one that year with 'Crying'. He took to the stage, sang the hit that the salesforce had helped to the top of the chart and then walked off. I took up the microphone to call him back for an encore and maybe a burst of 'American Pie' or 'Vincent' but nothing happened. I encouraged the crowd to call for him to come back but the shouts fell on stony ground, and then I spotted a colleague at the back of the room signalling frantically that there was to be no comeback. He was doing a cutting motion across his throat and pointing out of the hotel's front door as if to say 'Don's gone' ... and sure enough he had. After just one number, he had fled the room, got into a limo and rushed back to Central London, presumably to have more fun than he was having in Slough with EMI's salesforce.

But what artists often failed to realise was that events like that were rarely forgotten by the people who sold their records and sure enough McLean never had a major UK hit after that. No self-respecting sales person was going to waste their time on a man who jilted them after one song - even if it was a number one.

Torquay was the venue for an important conference footie match between EMI office staff and the salesforce and, despite being retired many years, I came out to appear in goal - it was a position I had never played in before but by now midfield dynamo was beyond me.

We recruited my fellow Aston Villa fan Nigel Kennedy to play but the maestro of the violin was not so inspirational

- he proved to be more fiddler than dribbler - as the sales team thrashed us something like 7-1.

If money was tight in Slough for the first sales get-together after EMI had bought United Artists for $3million, there were no such concerns when it came to the EMI Worldwide Managing Directors conference held at the Gleneagles Hotel in Scotland in I think 1987.

For reasons that still baffle me we hired a company which was based in San Francisco and run by two Englishmen to organise a conference in Scotland and to add to the bizarre arrangement, the EMI people charged with coordinating it all were both based in London at the EMI Music Worldwide head office. I was one of those people and, as luck would have it, I had to fly to San Francisco for meetings to plan the event when EMI's most senior executives from around the world would meet up for close to a week.

The delegates' journey began in London when we hired the Queen's official train to travel up to York where we boarded a famous steam train which, we were reliably informed by those in the know, had never been to Scotland before. This brought out hordes of train spotters along the way as we journeyed direct to the hotel's own station. Along the way, the train stopped on the pretence of taking on water from some outpost or other but, while it was stationary, helicopters came into view and as they hovered nearby, ropes were dropped, fully armed soldiers climbed down and set about boarding the train. Known only to a select few, we had recruited an army regiment to use this as a training exercise which threw delegates into shrieks of either delight or panic.

However, it all ended peacefully enough with the commanding officer climbing aboard to present a box of chocolates ("the lady loves Milk Tray") to our only female

MD. And part of the deal was that we let the soldiers join us for dinner and have a night in the 5 star hotel.

During the week's activities - which included golf, shooting and archery tournaments, alongside some actual business presentations and performances from Nigel Kennedy and Bobby McFerrin - we flew in from Glasgow by helicopter Tina Turner and Brian May and Roger Taylor from Queen. And we got all this - plus a trip to a local distillery and complimentary bottles of vintage aged whisky - for a mere £500,000! Who said the music industry had more money than sense?

Although I can't remember where it was, the last EMI Records conference I attended - as a special EMI Music guest – has a place in my memory for a reason that has nothing to do with records or artists.

Bhaskar Menon, longtime head of Capitol in America and chairman of EMI Music Worldwide for a decade, was due to give a state of the nation address to the troops but on the morning in question was nowhere to be seen. Our head of Human Resources stood in to read his speech, explaining that Menon had been called away.

When I next met with Menon, I asked him about his hasty departure and enquired if everything was alright with his family. A little sheepishly, he explained that he had received a call from his tax adviser telling him that the IRS were on his case for an unreturned tax form and that he had 24 hours to get back to California and put everything in order. Not realising how severe the American tax authorities could be, I sort of laughed it off which prompted Menon to look at me and say, "Brian, when it comes to tax demands, we can safely assume that my earnings, investments and tax liabilities are far greater than your own." And of course they were as he had been an extremely well paid record executive - as head of EMI India, Capitol Records and EMI Music - for nigh-on twenty years.

Chapter 11

CHAPERONING MISS BUSH

It's interesting to think that EMI's decision to sign teenage prodigy Kate Bush in 1976 was perhaps sparked by the company losing million-selling American artists such as The Eagles, Stevie Wonder and Neil Diamond as the company shed its American licensing deals with the likes of Elektra/Asylum, Motown and MCA. The focus of attention now, as were told in no uncertain terms, was to find new homegrown British talent to follow in the footsteps of major artists such as Cliff Richard, Shadows, Beatles, Pink Floyd, Queen and T Rex.

Nobody knew it at the time but Kate Bush was going to revitalise the company fortunes – both in terms of sales and image – alongside a handful of punk and new wave acts. My boss Bob Mercer was involved with all the acts on the company's roster, none more so than Pink Floyd whose multi-million selling *Dark Side Of The Moon* album, in no small way, contributed to all our wages.

It was during a visit to Abbey Road Studios to hear tracks from the follow-up album *Wish You Were Here*, that Mercer was played a demo of Kate's which Floyd's guitarist Dave Gilmour had paid for in 1975 when she went into AIR

Studios in London with producer Andrew Powell. Suitably impressed with the compositions 'Man With A Child In His Eyes' and 'The Saxophone Song', Mercer set the wheels in motion to eventually sign Bush to EMI at around the time of her 18th birthday in July 1976. Having heard the demos made a year earlier in AIR (which was launched by Beatles producer George Martin), Mercer was keen to play them to anyone who would listen.

We were all surprised, excited and, most of all, astounded that these songs could have been written by a 15-year-old schoolgirl. We learned that it was through Dave Gilmour that she had arrived at EMI, and there were some who thought that she was signed as a sop to keep the Floyd superstar happy.

We wanted more details and somewhere along the line we got a fanciful story that the person who walked Gilmour's dog knew someone who knew Kate and they, in turn, had passed on some rough demos to the guitarist. Sadly this wasn't true and gradually we learnt that, in fact, it was a record plugger friend of Kate's brother John who had passed a tape to his old Cambridge friend Gilmour. The dog walker friend of a friend was always a more romantic story to my mind.

I was still head of press when Kate began coming into the office. Even though she wasn't officially signed to the company and she had no recordings for my press office to promote, I was introduced to her by Bob Mercer. However, she became a regular visitor to our Manchester Square offices, and as my office was opposite Mercer's and close to the A&R department, which worked most closely with her, our paths often crossed.

After making the move into artist development I was assigned the task of helping her along the way and, hopefully, putting her on the road to stardom. As a first step, Kate decided to take her newly formed KT Bush Band on a tour of London pubs and clubs in the spring of 1977 and I drove down to, I think, the Rose of Lee pub in the south London district of Lewisham to catch a performance. It was there that I met Kate's wonderfully eccentric mother Hannah who plied me with sausages (non-vegetarian thankfully) from the buffet table as she questioned me about my role in EMI's grand plan for her daughter. The gig took place in the corner of a bar where Kate and her bandmates - Del Palmer, Vic King and Brian Bath - played, as a I recall, covers of Beatles numbers (I'm sure 'Come Together' was in there) and Motown classics plus a few tunes I didn't recognize. Those tunes were probably early versions of songs written by Kate, with which I would become more familiar in the coming months.

The show that night was good, the band were more than adequate and Kate gave an energetic and surprisingly theatrical performance.

At the end I drove back excitedly into central London to the Royal Garden Hotel in Kensington where there was a reception for the Shadows who were celebrating selling a million copies of their *20 Golden Greats* album. I went there to find Bob Mercer, and a few other colleagues, to tell them that, ten miles away in what we rudely called 'sarf of the river', I had just witnessed some moments of magic.

While I wasn't party to the exact details of Bush's EMI deal - there was always some secrecy, even internally, about advances, royalties and the length of a contract - I was aware that, thanks to Mercer she was given 'special' treatment. This included a £3,000 advance along with some advice about honing her song writing.

As we all got used to hearing more and more of Kate's

music, a decision was made to try and calm things down a bit.

She was a prolific songwriter and, as we were all told in no uncertain terms by Mercer, she was 'an album artist' and not a two minute pop wonder, there was a need for her to write less not more ... quality not quantity if you like. Kate was given new tape recording equipment and eventually a brand new piano in order to hone her skills as a songwriter. Unusually for a giant commercial enterprise like EMI Records, there was no pressure on our new signing to produce a three minute hit single.

The choice of Andrew Powell as producer was a decision made, I think, between Kate and Dave Gilmour. Powell had been the musician, producer and arranger who had completed the original Gilmour-financed demos. He was also known to us through his work alongside producer Alan Parsons on hit acts such as Cockney Rebel and Pilot.

In the midst of all this activity, there were conversations a-plenty with Kate about her songs, her style and her ambitions.

Outwardly the teenage Kate Bush gave off an air of sixties hippie-dom and mystical disinterest but we learned soon enough that we were dealing with a determined young lady with a strong hold on her career and her business. Any idea we had that this industry novice might be a pushover was very soon dispelled.

Work on her debut album began in AIR's Studios, way above Oxford Circus in central London and, wearing my artist development hat, I made a number of trips down from Manchester Square to keep tabs on proceedings. Fortunately, I wasn't expected to do anything other than listen and nod as Powell and the musicians he had hired - Ian Bairnson and David Paton from Pilot, plus Cockney

Rebel's Stuart Elliott and Duncan Mackay - started to create the album.

The visits were usually fun and always friendly – I knew all four musicians from their previous EMI incarnations – and Kate was happy to chew the fat with 'the man from the record company'. Powell's enthusiasm led him to share quite freely the music they were creating during the summer of 1977.

Going into the autumn of 1977 we finally got a chance to hear the fully finished 13 track album that was to become *The Kick Inside*, although I don't recall any meetings to discuss the album's title or its artwork. I'm sure Bush had both of these things figured out from the outset although we almost certainly had to point out the 'must haves' when it came to an artist's early albums.

Years ago when I bought albums in record shops, very few artists had their own browser section, it was simply divided into Male/Female/Groups although Elvis, Frank Sinatra and Cliff and the Shadows might have had a bin to themselves. But then along came The Beatles and the Stones and within a couple of years they, plus probably Bob Dylan, the Beach Boys, Ray Charles and maybe even the Monkees, were separated from the rest of the albums. One of the rules back then was that both the artist's name and the album title were displayed prominently on the cover - top right corner was best for the name of the act - and that rang true for most releases although the Stones didn't put their name on their first album, even before The Beatles went 'nameless' for the first time on *Rubber Soul* in 1965. By contrast Pink Floyd played along for their first three albums, although they blatantly did the opposite with later covers.

Kate decided that her debut album would feature a

photo taken by American photographer Jay Myrdala of her strapped to a sort of dragon kite with oriental style lettering - which was fine with us. Nobody thought it was going to be a big seller so we didn't worry about the cover artwork - but we had to insist that name and album title went top right so it was easily accessible as potential buyers flipped through the Female Artists A-D section.

Somewhere in the midst of all this, I moved on to my third EMI job in that particular year. After Head of Press and Artist Development Manager, I became a marketing person and one of the acts that I was responsible for was Kate Bush. I was also involved in campaigns for artists such as Queen, Alfalfa, the Tom Robinson Band, Cliff Richard and the newly signed Rolling Stones.

While Kate had decided what her album was going to be called and what it would look like, the question of which track would be her debut single was still up in the air. There was a general feeling within EMI that it should be 'James And The Cold Gun' – which Bob Mercer described as "clever and more accessible" – while Kate was in favour of the unique and slightly weird sounding 'Wuthering Heights.'

The discussions with Kate were never heated and our view was that, as she was seen as an album artist who would probably need a couple of albums under her belt before we saw any real return on our investment and her hard work, the choice of first single didn't really matter. We all assumed it was never going to be a major hit anyway as it was the first record from a brand new unknown artist. So, on the basis that we didn't really mind, and Kate was adamant, 'Wuthering Heights' was scheduled for release on November 4th 1977.

And as the original release date got closer, and in line with the usual procedure, I took 'Wuthering Heights' down to the factory to play to the singles sales girls to see whether we'd got a Hit, Miss or even the dreaded 'shit' combination. In fact, as with 'Mull Of Kintyre', we got a Miss, so once again the girls we employed to sell our records were not convinced, but once again it didn't matter one iota. However, things changed as the demand for singles and albums pressed at EMI's plant in Hayes in the run-up to Christmas gathered momentum.

Following David Soul's No.1, 'Silver Lady' (licensed through Private Stock) and La Belle Epoque's hit 'Black Is Black' on Harvest, Queen delivered their block-buster anthem 'We Are The Champions' and Tom Robinson's '2-4-6-8 Motorway' climbed the charts.

At the same time EMI's new TV-advertised releases *20 Golden Greats* from Diana Ross and the Supremes and Cliff Richard's *40 Golden Greats* were both topping the album charts and they were all taking up valuable pressing capacity.

And there was another record lurking in the background which finally convinced us to move the release date of Kate's first single into 1978. While some of us had doubts about the song's pop credibility, we did all know deep down that Paul McCartney's Wings single 'Mull Of Kintyre' was going to be a hit and having it scheduled for release on November 13th was enough to convince us that Kate's debut record was just going to get lost - both in terms of airplay and sales.

While 'Mull Of Kintyre' was topping the UK chart for nine weeks from December to February 1978 and becoming the first British single to sell over two million copies, an extraordinary situation arose with 'Wuthering Heights' which none of us had foreseen.

Even though we had delayed the release of the single

and removed it from the pressing schedule, copies were produced and inadvertently delivered from the EMI factory to key radio and television stations, plus producers and journalists via what was dubbed the 'Automatic Mailing List'.

Now we had a problem. Nobody wanted a record that was not released or available in the shops, to be played on radio, however small the demand might be.

For the first time in my forty plus years in the record business, we sent our promotion staff out on a unique mission - to get the single back and stop it being played on radio. To a large extent the plan worked as most producers and disc jockeys were more than happy to return or ignore a first record by someone they had never heard of. However, there were two people at one station who refused to play ball.

Tony Myatt had a late night show on London's *Capital Radio*, produced by Eddie Pumer, and the two of them were adamant that not only were they not going to return the single but they were going to carry on playing it throughout November and December and all the way into 1978 – in fact, right through to its new official release date on January 20. Thanks to Myatt and Pumer, 'Wuthering Heights' became something of a phenomenon as listeners to Capital rang in to find out who Kate Bush was and when the record would be available. Their exact words to me were that their switchboard "lit up like a Christmas tree" with callers wanting the record.

Within two weeks of its release, on February 11 1978, 'Wuthering Heights' became a hit, entering the British singles chart at No.42, beginning a steady climb up the charts that culminated in it reaching the No.1 spot on March 7, where it stayed for a month. And nobody was more surprised than us - the team of so-called record experts that ran EMI at the time. Having said that, we were happy to take any credit that was thrown our way.

The most important music programme on British television in the mid-seventies was still the BBC's *Top Of The Pops* and it was important to us that Kate was featured and that the show's producer was keen to feature the UK's newest and brightest star. It was usual for a TV promotion person to go to the taping of the show but on this occasion I went to the TV Centre with Kate and, sadly, it was a less than pleasing experience.

Even though Kate had a band – and they were there at the studio – 'Wuthering Heights' was issued as a solo record and under BBC regulations and Musicians Union rules she would have to sing along to a backing track recorded by the BBC orchestra.

I remember that she was a very unhappy young lady that day, a time when she should have been enjoying her first taste of success. She battled through, sensibly realising that walking out was not going to achieve anything other than upsetting the powers-that-be at the Beeb which was never a wise thing to do. They held all the cards and perhaps it was our mistake that nobody had explained how it worked at *Top Of The Pops* - after all the rules hadn't changed in years regarding solo singers and backing musicians. Despite her anguish at her first appearance on *Top Of The Pops*, when 'Wuthering Heights' first broke into the required Top 40 bracket at No.27, she did return a few weeks later to give a much more assured and confident account of herself as the No.1 artist.

In the midst of the single's success, we had to attend to the small matter of releasing Kate's debut album *The Kick Inside* and go about creating a campaign that would take her into the hearts and ears of album buyers. To do that we knew we needed a strong image - something stronger than the cover shot of Bush clinging to a giant painted dragon kite.

When I moved into marketing, the man who took over my role as Kate's adviser in Artist Development was John Bagnall and he had the idea of hiring experienced rock photographer Gered Mankowitz to shoot the up-and-coming star. He had an eye on possible imagery for singles bags and maybe music trade magazine advertising, depending on how things went.

Mankowitz, who had already photographed Jimi Hendrix, the Stones and Small Faces, produced a collection of pictures with Kate in pink and green leotards and we welcomed them with enthusiasm ... here was a set of stunning photographs which we could use - and use them we did. They showed Bush as a frail and wide-eyed innocent teenager who was also stunningly attractive, and while Mankowitz delivered a series of pictures, showing her full length, three quarter length and portrait, somewhere along the line everything focused on a shot of Bush in a pink leotard which was cropped to show her nipples. I don‘t recall anyone being particularly shocked by the photograph, hundreds of young women supported the 1970s 'burn the bra' campaign and nobody viewed it as being exploitative or sexist. Bizarrely, I don't even remember who made the final decision about which shot we would use in a poster campaign aimed at promoting *The Kick Inside*, but I'm positive we wouldn't have gone ahead without explaining it to Kate by showing her the posters we had in mind to use. it was unlikely that Kate herself would have a problem, as she never seemed to have any concerns about her body at all. Her reaction was along the lines of "we (women) have all got those things" and a few weeks after the album came out she was quoted as saying, "I suppose the poster is reasonably sexy just 'cos you see my tits but I think the vibe from the face is there."

Her lack of concern - or maybe it was naivety - about her body, put me in an embarrassing spot when I was urging her to get ready to go along to an awards ceremony. She was in the small studio at Manchester Square doing something and I said, "Come on Kate, get a move on. There's a car outside." At which point she just took her top off - there was no bra - to change into something fancy without any hint of self-consciousness, while I stood in the corner quivering with my hands covering my eyes – well almost!

It's only fair to point out that by the mid-eighties, Kate had had a re-think and found the poster shots "quite embarrassing" and admitted that they probably should have been cropped differently. But, without any protest from the artist at the time, we ploughed on with the February 28 release of the album and a campaign which involved the use of the photo of Kate in a pink leotard with her name and the album title above her image with the superlatives WONDROUS, AMAZING or MAGNIFICENT below. Some were designed to fit the corners of London buses while other full-size posters went up in underground stations and on billboards. The posters did cause some controversy with, if I remember, both the *Daily Express* and *Private Eye* making some comments about decency, but, along with the success of 'Wuthering Heights', they did the trick. The album entered the chart in mid-March, peaked at No.3 and hung around for a total of 70 weeks while the follow-up single 'The Man With A Child In His Eyes' peaked at No.6 in June.

The delivery of Kate Bush to the British public had taken a first giant step thanks to her extraordinary talent and a set of simple yet powerful photographs taken by Mankowitz. Her dynamic UK success was repeated throughout Europe and as far away as Australia, New Zealand and Japan where Mankowitz's 'infamous' pink leotard shot was adopted for the album cover but cropped differently – without nipples!

But Kate's attractiveness and what I considered to be a complete lack of concern about her body and suggestions of sensuality did lead her and EMI into a brief moment of difficulty. Somehow, perhaps due to naivety on her part, she was persuaded by a Dutch photographer to pose for a picture where she was tied up in a microphone cable. As it circulated, the photograph began to be dubbed as a 'bondage shot' which, I remember, upset her. Our efforts to buy the photographs to stop their distribution failed and the shot appeared in Britain's *Record Mirror* music paper. Everyone involved saw it as a warning to be more careful about how Kate was presented in the media.

Mankowitz was also responsible for the album's cover shot for release on EMI America in the US, where the 'nipple shot' was, according to our American colleagues, considered seriously inappropriate. Still titled *The Kick Inside*, Mankowitz shot Bush inside a crate wearing a check shirt, jeans and leggings. Sadly, despite the new cover and Kate making a first brief promo trip to the States in May 1978, the album failed to chart in the US.

America was the biggest market in the world for recorded music and we, at EMI UK, and our counterparts in the US, were both desperate to find a way to crack 'the States'. Sadly, and surprisingly, Kate was never that bothered about world domination – especially if it involved flying, which she hated. Despite her disinterest, we readily agreed to a plan hatched up by the people at our American label. They had negotiated her the opening slot on the final leg of Fleetwood Mac's *Rumours* tour in the summer of 1978 which would take in large parts of the US. The opening spot on a tour headlined by one of the world's biggest-selling bands - the *Rumours* album would go on to sell almost 40 million copies worldwide - meant Bush would get around 20 minutes playing time, limited rehearsal and any fancy ideas involving jugglers and dancers were out of the question.

Unsurprisingly, Kate said no, telling us and America that she did not and would not present her music to anyone "in 20 minutes". She also refused a proposal to play three nights at New York's prestigious Radio City Music Hall where she would showcase her music to US media and industry big-wigs. To her credit she never complained to any of us about not selling records in America, where she eventually debuted on the chart at No.85 in March 1979 with 'The Man With A Child In His Eyes.'

Along with Bob Mercer and a few others others, I had many a vegetarian meal with Kate - that's one of the things we record people did... buy lunches and dinners for artists while flying the company flag - and one of things on the menu alongside nut cutlets, rissoles and roasted vegetables was who was going manage Kate Bush. Artist Development had done its work as she hit the charts and grew into her role as a best-selling artist but we all thought an actual manager would help take her to the next step.

The obvious choice was Steve O'Rourke who managed Pink Floyd, including Dave Gilmour, but he didn't fancy the job. Then we approached Peter Lyster-Todd, who looked after Sky the instrumental rock group led by guitarist John Williams, but that also proved to be a non-starter. There was even a brief moment when we considered asking Tony Howard, who had managed Marc Bolan and Tom Robinson, but his gruff, sometimes abrasive manner was never going to work with Miss Bush.

So she settled on a sort of do-it-yourself arrangement through her company Novercia (the Latin translation is 'new woman') which handled her management and music publishing. It involved members of her family including brothers John (a photographer and poet) and Paddy (an instrument maker and musician) alongside experienced music industry lawyer Bernard Sheridan. And we continued to help out both domestically and internationally when and where required.

One thing which didn't involve the family was the host of music industry awards she was collecting along the way as Best Female Singer, Best Newcomer and for Best Single. It turned out that my job was to accompany Bush to these award ceremonies as, for reasons I'm not quite sure of, it was decided that she should not admit to going out with - and certainly not living with - her bass-playing beau Del Palmer. She might drop a hint about seeing someone not in the music industry while all the time dismissing any talk of heavy relationships or marriage.

So there I was, a sort of unofficial stand-in for her boyfriend, at all these fancy events, chaperoning the biggest new name in British music as she revelled in the attention she received from the likes of Michael Palin and Rowan Atkinson, who were star guests at various award shows. My role involved a certain amount of protection, especially on occasions when her naivety came to the fore. At the *Melody Maker* Awards in November 1978 - when she won Best Female Vocalist and Brightest Hope - I had to rescue her from the clutches of two wild Irish rock legends as my mate Philip Lynott and his pal Bob Geldof moved in to try and woo Ms Bush with their best lines.

'Boyfriend' or bodyguard, Brian Southall keeps an eye on Kate Bush

There was also a trip abroad when I accompanied her, my managing director Ramon Lopez and EMI's International Manager (later to become Kate's personal manager) Hilary Walker, to Italy when we hired a private jet to take us to San Remo in January 1979 for a televised appearance at the legendary song festival. Kate was nervous about the flight and her performance as a non-competing singing guest, alongside Tina Turner, Chic and Demis Roussos. She got through versions of 'Hammer Horror' and 'Wow', two songs from her second album *Lionheart*, and then, in the style of Elvis, we left the building pronto to return home the same day.

Kate may have been riding on the crest of a very big wave with the, almost, global success of her first singles and debut album but the follow-up beckoned. It was in late

1978 that the first rumblings about her going on tour began, but we had to weigh up that opportunity against the need to release some new music and capitalise on what we had achieved so far.

Even though she was a prolific writer, she had been forced to write the music for her follow-up album in the midst of huge demands in terms of promotion and publicity. The recording of *Lionheart* took place in Superbear Studios near Nice in southern France during the summer of 1978 with overdubs and mixing in September and October with Andrew Powell once again acting as producer. This time however, Bush was credited as assistant producer.

Gered Mankowitz was called on again, this time to shoot the album cover, and he followed a brief set out by Kate of her being a child in an attic, finding a dressing up box and putting on a lion bodysuit. Gered also delivered a stunning back cover portrait of Bush.

The title of the album came from the track 'Oh England, My Lionheart' and the image gave us something to work with in terms of advertising. However, still wearing my marketing hat, I managed to upset Mankowitz by allowing the cover shot to be cropped into a triangle shape, following the lines of the attic window and the light reflection on the opposite wall.

While it gave us the opportunity to create interesting and eye-catching shaped posters, I did it without consulting Gered Mankowitz who was a bit pissed off at what I had done.

A few years on, when I reminded him of his displeasure, Mankowitz thankfully had forgotten he was ever upset - indeed he didn't remember that I had bastardised his photographs to create triangular posters. I'm delighted to say that we are still friends.

Me, far left and fuzzy, watching over proceedings at Kate Bush's Lionheart album signing session

EMI decided to go all international for the launch of *Lionheart* by hiring the 14th century Ammersoyen Castle in the Netherlands as the venue for a glitzy party attended by Kate and her family; EMI executives from the UK, Europe and Canada (interestingly execs from EMI's sister US company were either not invited or chose not to make the trip), major media (including Tony Myatt and Eddie Pumer), but NOT, it seems, Gered Mankowitz who, for some inexplicable reason was not on the guest list.

Despite the fanfare, *Lionheart* was not as successful as we all hoped, but then again we knew from bitter experience that the second album from a new artist was invariably a tough sell. Often they were rushed both in terms of writing and recording, released without proper consideration in an effort to cash in on the momentum of a successful debut release, or were just too different from what the public had to come to expect.

Maybe everybody was guilty on all three counts. Either way, *Lionheart*, released in November, peaked at number six in December 1978 after the single 'Hammer Horror' had stalled at No.44, ahead of the second single 'Wow' climbing to No.14 in April 1979 - boosted by Kate's all-important 28 date tour of the UK.

With a 13-strong cast of dancers, musicians and a magician, plus glorious set designs, the *Tour Of Life* kicked off at the Liverpool Empire on April 3 1979 and I was there to "fly the EMI flag and buy dinner" for cast and crew alike. In fact I think we all ate relatively cheaply in the hotel, without Kate.

After rounds of drinks in the bar, magician Simon Drake entertained us with his close-up magic - and I reminded him, to his great embarrassment, of the days when I knew him as a young record plugger at rival record company Decca. It had been a great first night and an extraordinary showcase for Kate's music - and I knew straight away that she had cast the die and set her own standards as far as live work was concerned. Despite being very nervous about making her professional debut, she was never going to compromise by taking a support spot on any major act's tour, playing dates in small clubs or following the traditional rock 'n' roll blueprint.

After *Lionheart*, I moved on within EMI to become head of corporate PR, with added responsibility for a while for the company's TV and radio promotion team, and was delighted to receive a personal thank you message from Kate. She signed a framed copy of *The Kick Inside* pink leotard poster with the words: *To dear dear Brian. Thank you a million for all your help and the times it's hurt from laughing with you. Lots of Love Kate xxxx.* It still hangs on a wall in my house as a reminder of the good times.

My signed poster from Kate Bush

It was during this time in my new role that I took myself off to Abbey Road to see how Kate was getting on with her 1982 album *The Dreaming*. She was somewhere in the middle of recording and producing the title track, highlighting the plight of Australian Aborigines, when I arrived. It was also the day when the Australian instrument the didgeridoo was delivered and Rolf Harris had been invited in to play it. Bush wanted to play the unique wind instrument herself but was told that under Aboriginal law women weren't allowed to. Disappointed but not keen to go against thousands of years of tradition, she accepted the situation and looked on as Harris made his contribution which included teaching brother Paddy Bush how to play it.

Although it reached No.3 in the UK album chart, *The Dreaming* was given a mixed reception in the music press with *Melody Maker* describing it as "bewildering". Future Pet Shop Boy (and EMI artist) Neil Tennant wrote in *Smash Hits* that it was "very weird."

Even before the album came out, there were misgivings around EMI about its commercial appeal. I think there was a point when the company even considered rejecting it and returning it to the artist to "do better." There were clauses in recording contracts which gave the record company the right to refuse an album and I think this was the closest EMI ever got to returning an album during my time there.

Over the years, Kate and I exchanged notes and Christmas cards - many of which I have kept along with those from Queen, the Pet Shop Boys, Cliff Richard and Iron Maiden - but, as with most relationships that are based on business more than friendship, you lose contact. It's nobody's fault and there are few if any recriminations and I was delighted to get offered tickets (to be paid for) for her 22-date residency at the Hammersmith Odeon in 2014. I was amused to see that she was still reluctant to travel too far and was never going to get into the rigours and cost of carting a crew and set around the country. The shows predictably sold out in minutes and, in true Kate Bush style, I saw a show that was both brilliant and bonkers – I wouldn't have expected anything else.

And, as one who was never going to play the game in the traditional way, she didn't show up at the after-show event - a drinks and nibbles get-together - where I waited patiently across the room from actor Tom Hollander and director and writer Richard Curtis. In all honesty I never expected her to show but it would have been great just to say 'hi' one more time.

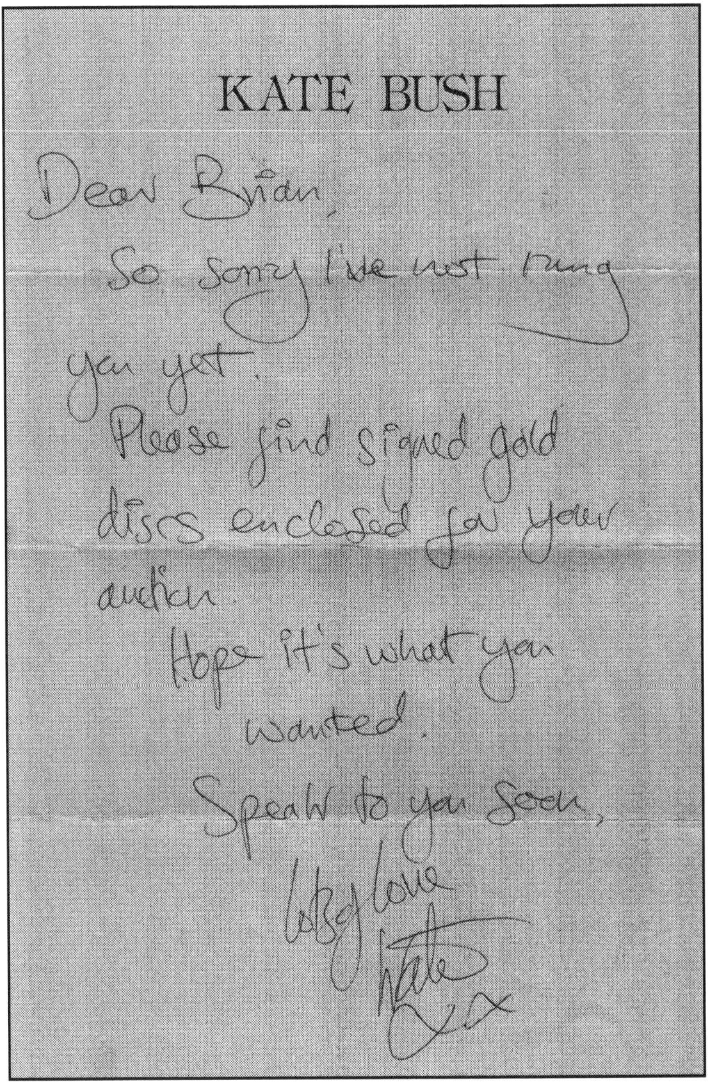

KATE BUSH

Dear Brian,

So sorry I've not rung you yet.

Please find signed gold discs enclosed for your auction.

Hope it's what you wanted.

Speak to you soon,

Lots of love

Kate xx

Above: Kate Bush's letter came with some gold discs for the author's charity

Left: Christmas greetings to the author from Kate

Chapter 12

'HAVE I GOT A BAND FOR YOU!'

On the back of signing Kate Bush, there were some serious attempts to add to the roster and her producer Andrew Powell was one act we signed. There was a thought that by signing him we might get near to getting the Alan Parsons Project which was led by a former EMI staffer and producer of hits for Pilot and Cockney Rebel. It didn't work out and Powell's single album didn't make much of an impact.

There were other scenarios involving artists we signed in the hope of some success coming from their famous connections. Singer John Christie came to us thanks to Dave Clark (he of the DC5) who produced his single 'Time Of Our Lives' which failed to register, while David Austin's single 'Turn To Gold' was co-written by his close friend George Michael and, despite our high hopes, it peaked at No.68.

During my time, unsuccessful talks were held with David Essex - apparently there were concerns about who was going to write the songs, Robin Gibb - in the hope that we might get the Bee Gees - and I brought my mate Philip Lynott and Thin Lizzy into the frame but, despite our long friendship, nothing came of it. Then there was a supreme effort to sign Elton John who was managed by the same John Reid who managed Queen. I'm not sure how far the negotiations went but they all fell apart when Elton or Reid demanded a key man clause in the contract relating to the two most senior executives in EMI Music Worldwide. I was told that they wanted a firm commitment that these two men would not leave the company for a good few years or maybe even the length of the contract on the table. Nobody at our new bosses, Thorn EMI, was going to agree to that and sure enough Elton never arrived and both of the execs went within a couple of years.

We were successful in signing Duran Duran, when the fact that keyboard player Nick Rhodes was the nephew of Peter Laister, the head of Thorn EMI, sparked rumours about a deal. It's certainly true that Laister, whose daughter is now manager of Duran Duran, made a call pointing out that a demo tape by the band had been with the company's A&R people for a while without anything happening. Proving that sometimes who you know is as important as what you play, it all worked out in the end as the band notched up close to 30 hit singles and eight chart albums in nearly two decades with us. They weren't my favourite band musically, although both Nick Rhodes and John Taylor were charming and accessible while singer Simon Le Bon could be an ass at times. We almost came to blows close to Christmas one year when there was a silly confrontation over a poster which he kept pushing into my chest and I kept brushing away. As it got more heated, and the pushing on both sides got more vigorous, somebody stepped in and life went back to normal.

Duran's John Taylor (right) doesn't seem too interested in the advice he's getting from me

Having signed with EMI, Nick Rhodes then brought us a band whose singer he had met as a waiter in a London restaurant. Kajagoogoo, led by Limahl, proved their worth with seven hit singles (including a No.1) and a Top 10 album, which just goes to prove that you get your hits however and wherever you can.

Following the departure of executives Leslie Hill and

Ramon Lopez, we found ourselves with a new MD in the shape of Cliff Busby who came with the deal to buy United Artists - a strange sort of two-fer. However, he only took charge after John Bush's brief time (a matter of weeks) as MD of EMI Records came to an abrupt end after some sort of record exporting scandal at his previous company (EMI Italy) was uncovered.

Busby had been an EMI salesman during the sixties and he had his own way of running the company and the answers you got depended on the time of day. After 'lunch' was not a good time to raise an important issue. He was brusque and very sweary and, comparing him with the gentlemanly way Lopez ran things, led me to explain to colleagues the difference between their negotiating skills. Asking the almost aristocratic Spanish intellectual Lopez for a raise was usually met with a 30-minute diatribe about world economics while Busby's stock response was to tell you to "f*** off".

In later life, when I was again working for Lopez, I actually took to writing the rate of inflation and retail price index figures on the palm of my hand so I was prepared for all eventualities.

It was Busby who brought us back together with our old friend, the Sex Pistols manager Malcolm McLaren, and his new band Bow Wow Wow, fronted by a 13-year-old girl singer, Annabella Lwin.

McLaren was again intent on creating a situation when he decreed that the band's first release – 'C30 C60 C90' – should be issued as the world's first cassette single. As I recall, we had many meetings about this idea and were never keen on it as it promoted home taping at a time when the music industry was going all-out with an anti-home taping campaign. There wasn't a lot of effort put into promoting the release but despite our admittedly half-hearted efforts the cassette (a regular vinyl single followed) did reach the UK Top 40. As with the Pistols, McLaren's obsession with creating a situation didn't result in his act having a lasting career with EMI.

The arrival of Cliff Busby and his team of UA executives also meant a recruitment drive on behalf of the Freemasons and the number within EMI almost doubled overnight. The music industry had been a haven for the Masons for years - their activities (which some considered to be dubious) even got a write-up in *Private Eye* on one occasion in the 1980s. We were all aware of the 'special' deals between the company's sales execs and the one-stop operations who supplied jukebox owners and small independent stores too small to qualify for record company accounts. *Private Eye*, like most of us, put down the links - and the deals that were done - to various Lodge meetings. But, despite the new boys best efforts to get us 'non-UA' people to join the 'club', very few signed up. As for me ... I never even got invited to audition for the Masons. Make of that what you will.

Buying United Artists meant their roster of best-selling acts came into the EMI fold and this included ELO (their Jet label was distributed by UA), Whitesnake, Don McLean, Gerry Rafferty, the Vapors and the Stranglers who, as I recall, were not altogether happy with their new label. There were apparently 'artistic differences' over the music they were making and despite the single 'Golden Brown' reaching No.2 in 1982, they found a way out the following year.

Convinced we didn't want them - and they didn't want to be with us - a deal was struck whereby they were able to leave and sign to the Epic label run by CBS, in return, I was told, for us getting a royalty payment (or 'override') on sales of any Stranglers' records that would have been made and released within their original UA/EMI contract before their move to CBS.

It's not often that a record label allows a successful act to leave and the Stranglers had racked up 13 UK hit singles and seven chart albums in four years between 1977 and 1981. They said their goodbyes to us with a greatest hits package which was then, and maybe still is, the industry's accepted method of an act fulfilling a contract before moving on. And please note that if an artist has to deliver two albums to fulfil their contract, then they will quickly produce a double live album.

The search for new talent also brought us Talk Talk who puzzled most of us with their extraordinary music and complete disdain for the music business and record companies even though they racked up nine chart singles and four chart albums - with *The Colour of Spring* hitting the Top 10 - between 1982 and 1988. Despite the success (and media acclaim) - although none of their original singles went higher than 14 - they were always a tough sell and made it clear that they were going to go their own way, swapping white New Romantics outfits for jeans and t-shirts. Even after I had spent a most enjoyable Friday night and Saturday morning with them in Birmingham for a TV show - probably *Tiswas* - when we discussed the merits of Susan Maughan's 1960s hit 'Bobby's Girl' (don't ask me why), things were still destined to end in tears when they decided not to release a single from the album *Spirit of Eden* and vowed not to tour. There were legal wranglings and eventually they left EMI with some litigation still up in the air.

One band who were close to an EMI contract but fell at the last fence were Culture Club who had actually made demos in EMI's studios in 1981. But things never progressed much further and the story that went round the company was that Boy George turning up in make-up with coloured dreadlocks and a feather boa was too much for one of EMI's senior A&R men and all bets were off.

What would have been interesting was to have had both Culture Club and Duran Duran on the same label. I don't know how they got on with each other as artists but there was certainly no love lost between their rival fans who regularly got into shouting matches when they turned up outside our offices and at Virgin Records where Culture Club were signed.

Described by some as a cyber-punk band, Sigue Sigue Sputnik were led by Tony James and came complete with leather, fishnet masks and colourful hair which made them, in my opinion, too pretty to be punks and not pretty enough to be New Romantics. We signed them in around 1984, when James told the press that we had paid a £4 million advance when it was in fact only £350,000, but he was never one to let the truth spoil a good story. He did, however, have a brand new unique marketing idea which involved selling advertising slots between the tracks on their album *Flaunt It*, and he managed to persuade a few companies to take 20 or 30 second spots for anything up to a reported £5,000. His plan aroused the interest of BBC Radio 1 and, as head of corporate PR for EMI Records by then, I was invited into the studio to give our reaction to the idea. I explained that we weren't necessarily against it but had some concerns about its validity and how the ads would sit with record buyers. Asked whether it was an idea that could be used on other releases, I asked on air which ads would go where and with which sort of music saying, "You wouldn't want a commercial for baked beans between

Beethoven's movements." And a couple of people back at the office even got the joke.

Although many of EMI's roster of rock stars were visitors (some more regular than others) to the offices, it was always a major disappointment that David Bowie - to the best of my recollection - never popped in for a chat. Certainly I never saw him.

He was signed for around $17 million by EMI America in the US in 1983 and delivered major hits such as 'Let's Dance', 'China Girl' and 'Modern Love' alongside chart topping albums *Let's Dance* and *Tonight*, but was not a man given to discussing tactics with his record company. The people within EM who looked after his releases, including my radio and TV promotion department, always dealt with Coco Schwab, his loyal, longtime assistant. She has been described as Bowie's "protector against intruders and external nuisances" and, although I'm not sure we fell into either of those brackets, we were kept at more than arm's length from the great man.

Chapter 13

ROLLING WITH THE STONES

The Rolling Stones came into my life for a third time in early 1977 when, in the aftermath of the Sex Pistols debacle, we signed the original bad boys of rock. After my meeting with them as a cub reporter in 1965 and being on tour with them and Billy Preston in 1973, I was disappointed that Jagger didn't remember me when they joined EMI.

Jagger, who explained that the band had signed with EMI because "in jubilee year I feel it is fitting that we sign with a British company", then warned our MD Leslie Hill that "if I go on television and say 'f***' you're not going to fire me". He never did so we didn't have to even if we had wanted to.

With the ink only just dry on the Stones' new six album distribution deal with EMI, Keith Richards got himself into a spot of bother in Canada when he was arrested in Toronto for possession of heroin and cocaine. But it was too late for the EMI top brass to step in and do anything to derail the deal even if they were tempted ... taking on the Stones would have been a lot more tricky than sacking the Pistols.

Barbara Charone, who went on to become press officer

to the stars, was working for *Sounds* and filed a story from Canada covering Richards' arrest. In the story published on March 12 1977, she wrote, "When questioned on future tour prospects (without Keith Richards) Brian Southall at EMI, who had only just signed them, said without hesitation, 'They'll probably have to get another guitarist'." And she finished with the pay off line "Tell that to Keith Richards."

This brought an immediate reaction from Jagger and their business manager Prince Rupert Loewenstein who both wanted me fired for giving such a foolish and unofficial comment.

My boss Bob Mercer called me in and asked me what the hell I was playing at and all I could tell him was that I didn't say it. Of course I had no proof of that and the only way I could prove my innocence was to ask the editor of *Sounds* (an old *Melody Maker* colleague of mine) to get some evidence from Charone either on tape or even a shorthand note that I said it, while at the same time suggesting that legal action might follow. When neither was forthcoming - and I was confident Charone would have no evidence to back up the mis-quote - I was off the hook and *Sounds* were forced to print an apology in the March 26 edition. It appeared under the heading 'Stones Correction' and carried on to clarify that regarding the quote attributed to Mr Brian Southall from EMI Records, "We would like to point out that the quote was incorrect and apologise to Mr Southall and EMI Records for any embarrassment caused."

So I was in the clear and over 18 months later Richards was also let off with a suspended sentence for the possession charges – and he didn't miss a gig so they didn't have to get another guitarist after all.

The Stones' first album for us was *Some Girls* and it showed two sides of the group and in particular Jagger, the acknowledged leader of the band. On the one hand Jagger was a stickler for detail and concerned himself with almost every aspect of the album cover design and marketing campaign.

We would get calls from America when an English voice, without any identification, would start talking about type sizes and pantones. Within minutes you realised it was Jagger and it turned out it was something he had done for years – and enjoyed.

On the other hand, the Stones courted controversy at every turn and the cover for *Some Girls*, so carefully created and designed, took us back into the realms of The Beatles and their *Sgt Pepper* album cover when they included images of people without their permission. Now the Stones did the same with a mock wig advertisement sleeve which featured Raquel Welch, Lucille Ball and Farrah Fawcett-Majors. They - and others - threatened legal action, so we had to come up with a new cover with the celebrity faces blanked out and the faces of the Stones in the cut-out holes.

Their next album *Emotional Rescue* came out in July 1980 and once again there was a hiccup in our launch plans. We, with the band's agreement, had arranged to have a launch party in the grounds of the Royal Hospital Chelsea and we gave it a 'MASH' theme with tents, tin plates and white surgical coats.

Food and drinks were ordered, the media and other relevant folk were invited and all was set for the off when a call came through on the morning of the party to say that the band were not going to make it. Why? We never found out, but we were certainly not going to let all the food go to waste so it was trucked back to Manchester Square where I arranged for it to be laid out in my office - it was quite a big office - for people to come and help themselves.

And even without a launch party, the album went to No.1 in the UK and US.

There was a clause in the Rolling Stones contract which stipulated how much money we had to spend marketing each of their album releases and it just went to show how arse about face things often were in the record business. With a Stones album - and a few other big name acts - you didn't need an expensive campaign, just a couple of adverts announcing the release, together with the usual accompanying single. That would normally do the trick to let fans know there was a new album out.

We could have simply stuck it in a brown paper bag, put an ad in *MM* or *NME*, slapped up an (illegal) poster on the streets and you had a campaign ... and the money allocated to the big name acts could have been spent on trying to break some new signings who, because they were new, didn't qualify for any significant marketing spend. That way, maybe, the likes of Alfalpha, No Dice, Albion Dance Band and Private Lives would not have ended up as either one hit or no hit wonders.

As part of the research for a book I was writing while at EMI (more about that later) I managed to blag a trip to Florida in October1981 to see the Stones at the Tangerine Bowl in Orlando. It was a magnificent sell-out event with a crowd of 120,000 and Van Halen as support. The gig apparently grossed $1.8million and no doubt a good chunk of that came from the extraordinary range of merchandise that was on sale which, I am glad to say, we managed to claim as freebie souvenirs.

Together with my EMI International pal John Cavanagh, we met up with Jagger the following day and while there was talk about singles and albums, there was no chance the great man was going to help me with my book research. But he did invite us to Bill Wyman's 45th birthday party which was set for Disney World - the band had taken it over either after closing time or had it closed so they could party with the group's most senior member. Sadly, the weather took a mighty turn for the worse and, with a hurricane forecast, the whole thing was cancelled.

The next episode involving the Stones was perhaps the oddest of all as it revolved around me possibly being hired to run their European operations. The job, which I didn't apply for and knew nothing about, involved liaising with their record companies (EMI and, in the US, Atlantic), promoters, agents, producers, sponsors, publishers and probably a host of other companies linked with the band's various operations and businesses. This left Prince Rupert to look after the money and, as I found out, conduct the initial interviews for the job from his fancy offices just off London Wall.

When I arrived to meet the Spanish-born German aristocrat, I was greeted by a butler who asked if I wanted coffee. When I said "yes please", he asked if I had a preference. "A little milk and no sugar" was my reply, which was when he asked again about my preference - "Jamaican, Brazilian or Sumatran?" Realising that Nescafe was not going to cut it, I opted for Jamaican ... and jolly good it was too.

The interview was fine, although there was a small hiccup when it came to money as I wanted more than they were offering which was not a lot more than I was getting at EMI. With that, the Prince, looking at my background in PR, suggested that the band could sack whoever was doing the press, give me that role (together with that person's money) in order to meet my demand.

All this sort of fell in with the industry's consensus that

Jagger was not in the business of splashing the cash. Hire one bloke, sack somebody else and give the first person almost, but not quite, two salaries... that made good business sense even to me. However, there was a sense of disappointment as I left the Prince's office when, after saying goodbye, he asked "Sorry, what was the name again?" I thought, now that's how to make a first impression.

I then discovered that I had been put forward for the job by my former boss Bob Mercer who, by now, was working for EMI Films where, we were delighted to hear, his expenses, after a lengthy stay in the Beverly Hills Hotel in Los Angeles, were an item for discussion at an EMI main board meeting. Good on you Bob, we thought. Nothing has changed.

Apparently, Bob had recommended two EMI people to Jagger and I was one of those on the very short list. The next step involved a phone call to my office at EMI which I answered with "hello" and, after I had confirmed that I was Brian Southall, the voice on the other end said, "It's Mick Jagger here."

My immediate reaction was that it wasn't him at all but my brother - who I had told I was in the frame for the Stones job - pretending to be the singer. I said "yeah", he said "yeah" and this went on for a few seconds before he mentioned that I had recently been to see Prince Rupert and now he wanted to see me. Suitably embarrassed, I said "yeah" again and we set a date for me to go to the Stones' office in Cheyne Walk in deepest Chelsea.

I immediately called my wife to tell her the story and explain that I had assumed that it was my brother making the call. That was when she said that Jagger had called my home phone number, she had answered and when he said who it was, she thought it was my brother as well.

Fortunately, it seemed that Jagger didn't hold this farcical turn of events against me as I went down to his office to discuss the job. On arrival I met him and Jerry Hall - and my, she was tall. As we chatted, it immediately became apparent that here was a man who knew all about record companies, marketing and promotion - and so he should, I thought, after two decades in the business.

But any idea I might have had about working for the Stones came to nothing. The other person in the frame for the position, my old colleague Colin Burn, was given the job on Mercer's final recommendation. Years later, he explained to me that he had only talked up Burn as he was going to be sacked from EMI and would be in need of a job - while I was safe in my executive role. I understood and bore no resentment towards either Mercer or Burn who, it has to be said, hated almost every minute of the job but stuck with it for almost a decade. Maybe I was well out of it, who knows?

Chapter 14

AUTHORING

Over the years I have written around 20 books and been lucky enough to have all of them published, some in hardback, some in paperback, some in both and two privately. As a former journalist, the ambition to actually write a book and then have people read it (preferably after they've bought it) was always there, although my debut as an author came to pass in slightly odd and unexpected circumstances.

Abbey Road Studios was opened in 1931 and as we approached its fiftieth anniversary in 1981, two men who worked there began researching a book of photographs tracing the studio's great history. Unfortunately Peter Vince and Allan Rouse couldn't find a publisher so I was asked to step in and try and arrange a publishing deal. I managed to get one with the independent publisher *Patrick Stephens (PSL)* but they wanted a proper book with words - around 50,000 or more - and pictures. And so it was that I was invited by the bosses of EMI Records to write the official history of the studio with the help of both Vince and Rouse.

Working from a long list of the great names who had recorded in the studio, I set about interviewing producers, engineers and artists and in 1982 the book *Abbey Road – the story of the world's most famous recording studios* - came out.

Looking back over 40 years later, I recall interviewing Paul McCartney in the place he used as his hideaway from his bandmates. Apparently, they each had one and his was in the boiler room which was where we talked one afternoon, seated on a couple of upturned crates in something like 80 degrees of heat. Then there was a delightful afternoon spent with George Martin and his wife Judy talking about their days at the studio – she was his secretary in the Parlophone office.

There were great stories – too many to mention here – but Tim Rice painted a glorious picture of being in the studio, where he worked with Norrie Paramor on Scaffold records, and having a canteen break when all four Beatles walked in. He recalled the moment, "I was speechless; there I was in the canteen on my own with The Beatles. I was overwhelmed while the girls behind the counter didn't seem the least bit concerned."

In the aftermath of The Beatles recording in the studio for almost a decade, the place became a sort of shrine for both the public and artists. Duran Duran did try to record their first single 'Planet Earth' there as drummer Roger Taylor recalled, "It was our first single and EMI suggested we use Abbey Road, we thought 'great Kate Bush, The Beatles ... they've used it so it should be good enough for us'." While it didn't quite work out for the Durans, Ms Bush was taken with the studio as she told me back then. "After a few days of recording there I realised that there is something very special about the place; it's a feeling, an aura if you like. It's built on ley lines which means there are very powerful forces at work."

Whether any ley lines run under Abbey Road I'm not sure but either way, Pink Floyd were less impressed as Dave Gilmour explained, "The myth about The Beatles and Studio Two didn't affect me - it's just a studio. It never occurred to me that The Beatles had used it."

However strongly The Beatles were connected to Abbey Road, it was interesting to talk to Lady Shirley Beecham, widow of the great English conductor Sir Thomas Beecham who began recording in Abbey Road during the 1930s. She recounted that her husband, who died in 1961, would not have been impressed with the arrival of the 'fab four' and their contemporaries. "He never paid any attention to music that wasn't classical and he would have made a great scene if he had been alive when classical sessions were moved out of the studios and took second place to pop."

We'll never know what Beecham would have made of a glove puppet taking up valuable studio time in Abbey Road, but producer Bob Barratt had the task of recording an album by Basil Brush and his 'handler' Ivan Owen. He told me he noticed that Owen's voice in the studio was different to the one he heard on the puppet's TV shows. When Barrett mentioned it, Owen went out to his car, got hold of Basil, brought him into the studio, sat down in the empty space and immediately came up with the right 'Basil' voice. Apparently, he had to have his hand up Basil for it to work.

Barratt was one of the 'house' producers who was still at EMI during my time – George Martin (Bernard Cribbins, The Beatles, Cilla Black) and Ron Richards (The Hollies, PJ Proby, Shane Fenton) had both left and Norrie Paramor (Helen Shapiro, Cliff Richard and The Shadows) had died, while Wally Ridley (Alma Cogan, Swinging Blue Jeans, Benny Hill) was still there.

These were all people with stories to tell and I had an

idea back in the eighties for a radio show where notable producers would be asked to name and talk about the best/favourite record they had made, but it was Wally Ridley's bizarre choice that put me off the idea. He picked a single called 'Mad Passionate Love' made by the 6 foot 7 inches tall Cockney actor Bernard Bresslaw who couldn't sing. Nevertheless, Ridley explained to me that the "combination of that silly voice and that romantic song appealed to me. I made the most out of very little." In fact it was a Top 10 hit in 1958, but I still couldn't bring myself to pitch the idea to the BBC.

While talking to Bob Barratt, who also produced Gene Vincent in Abbey Road, we touched on his role in EMI during the swinging sixties and it turned out that while George Martin was focusing on acts from Liverpool and Ron Richards was busy with Manchester, Bob was scouting around Birmingham and going as far as Wales to find new acts. "I signed Keith Powell and the Valets and Mike Sheridan and The Nightriders who became the Idle Race led by Jeff Lynne."

A Welsh act Bob discovered and produced for the Columbia label, where he worked for Norrie Paramor, was a group called the Cougars who made a guitar and drums version of Tchaikovsky's *Swan Lake* called 'Saturday Night At The Duck Pond'. It was a minor Top 40 hit in 1963 and I was able to tell him, almost twenty years later when we sat in Abbey Road, that I had bought it - and still have it. He was delighted as it seems he had never met anybody who had actually shelled out hard cash for the single.

One of the great pop producers who didn't actually work for EMI but was a frequent visitor to Abbey Road was Mickie Most, who made hits for Donovan and Herman's Hermits in EMI's north London studio.

Talking over the 'old' days at Abbey Road with hitmaker Helen Shapiro

Mickie told me about the day when he couldn't get into the studio to record his group The Animals. He explained that studio time was expensive in the mid-sixties at around £8 to £10 an hour and session times were set in stone.

"I wanted to record the Animals during their UK tour and wanted to start at eight in the morning at Abbey Road but they refused to open before 10am, so I had go to another studio," he said. "We started at 8 am and by 8.15 am we had done the first track 'House of The Rising Sun' and then we had two and three quarter hours to spare. So we made an album and, as it was £8 an hour, we completed the whole thing for £24 which was a good deal." It was indeed a good deal as the single he made in 15 minutes was a number one hit in both the UK and US where the album *The Animals*, which included the track, reached No.7 on the chart.

Before I asked Wally Ridley the question about his favourite record - and lost the will to carry on with the programme idea - I put the same question to Mickie Most. He was a man who, in the sixties and seventies, was involved with more than 100 UK hits and, although he said he didn't have a favourite, he did admit that he was always fond of Jeff Beck's 'Hi Ho Silver Lining'. "When I sat in the car park at my daughter's school waiting for her to come out of the disco, it was always the last record they played so that was quite nice." Bizarrely it was less of a favourite with Beck who often said he didn't like the record and rarely played it even though it was his second biggest chart hit - (No. 14 in 1967 and No.17 in 1972).

What I consider to be one of my major contributions to the Abbey Road book was persuading Iain Macmillan, the man who shot the cover photograph for The Beatles *Abbey Road* album, to let me have an 'alternative' photo for the book's front cover.

When I interviewed him, he gave me some background, "It was Paul's idea and I was given ten minutes around lunchtime to do it. I managed to take six shots."

He also explained how McCartney had chosen to remove his sandals - "it was a hot day" - for some shots which, among other so-called 'clues', led to the "Paul Is Dead" story.

The 'alternative' image Macmillan gave me for the cover showed The Beatles walking across the crossing in the opposite direction to the final album cover shot, with a double decker bus in the background. Sadly it only appeared on the original hardback and paperback editions before Apple won a claim for ownership of Macmillan's photographs and the shot was removed. It was replaced by a photo of the famous crossing with a bus in the background but sadly not a Beatle to be seen anywhere.

The *Abbey Road* book was launched with a lavish party in the world-famous Studio 2 - or 'The Beatles studio' as it was known - when my family joined a host of famous names, studio staff, including Peter Vince and Allan Rouse, and media people.

Chatting with BBC Radio One presenter Andy Peebles (right) at my Abbey Road book launch

Steve Van Zandt (2nd right) listens to some of my inside stories about Abbey Road

Alongside luminaries such as Sir Joseph Lockwood and Lady Beecham there were the producers George Martin, Wally Ridley and Alan Parsons, radio presenters Roger Scott and Andy Peebles, studio stalwarts Cliff Richard and Brian Bennett and Bruce Welch from the Shadows plus the visiting American musician Steve van Zandt (Little Steven) from Bruce Springsteen's band and *The Sopranos*. In addition to the party, there was also a special limited edition *Abbey Road* album which was sent out to radio and TV stations to help promote the book.

In fact, it was a very special limited edition as, I think only about 150 were pressed, and it was made up of hit singles recorded in the studio from 1954 through to 1977 – and they were almost all number ones from Eddie Calvert through to Wings.

And what made it even more special was the fact that it contained a chart-topping hit by The Beatles ('She Loves You') at a time when the group still steadfastly refused to release tracks for various artists' collections – other than Lennon's 1969 support for the World Wildlife Fund charity. There was even talk of releasing the album – with maybe a couple of tweaks (like removing The Beatles probably) – as a commercial album for sale to the public, but that fell apart when the researchers got to work.

By 1982 we were into the business of market research big-time when it came to TV advertised albums and the people in the know reported back from their various target groups that an album including hits from the 50s, 60s and 70s by singers like Ruby Murray, Cilla Black and Frank Ifield didn't sit well alongside groups such as Gerry and The Pacemakers, Manfred Mann or the Temperance Seven or later bands such as Pilot and Steve Harley & Cockney Rebel. It would have been nice to see it out there for the public to decide but it was not to be, although I still have a couple of copies in my collection and looking at it now, over 40 years on, I've noticed a curious omission on the cover which is a drawing of a bit of the famous zebra crossing leading to the official City of Westminster road sign Abbey Road NW8. On the wall behind the sign are the names of the artists, written in 'chalk' graffiti style, featured on the album ... minus one. There are 24 acts on the record and 23 names on the album cover and the unlucky act for some unknown reason is Peter and Gordon. As there was still space for another name it's fair to assume that they were just forgotten - such, as they say, is fame.

While the advance for the book went to Messrs Vince and Rouse (it was their idea after all) and the royalties went to EMI (it was their studio and I worked for them) my reward was an all-expenses paid trip around Britain to promote the book. The highlights were arriving in Leicester late one night to be told by the radio station that they had heard that I might have been killed in a car crash, and going on to Liverpool to the BBC station where they had no knowledge of me at all but were expecting a man called Patrick Stephens to talk about his *Abbey Road* book. Patrick Stephens, of course, was the publisher and I wondered if, when they had an author whose book was published by Penguin, did they expect to interview a penguin? And in Edinburgh, where I arrived after a late night drive from Leeds for a Saturday morning interview, we (me and the station) discovered that the show's host was at home drunk in bed. So I ended up interviewing myself ... and very good I was too.

But it wasn't just the regions who were anxious to talk to me about the *Abbey Road* book as BBC Radio Two stalwarts Gloria Hunniford and Pete Murray both invited me on for a chat in late 1982.

The Pete Murray show was his *Saturday Night Late Late* programme which went out somewhere around midnight and I was booked for the same Saturday as I was in Edinburgh for the unexpected self-interview. This meant a hurried flight back from Scotland, my wife Pat collecting me at the airport and then driving into central London to talk to Mr. Murray - and it soon became apparent that he hadn't read the book or, if he had, he'd forgotten most of it. Nevertheless these were rosier days at the BBC and unexpectedly I received a cheque for £27 for his show and a further £10 for Gloria Hunniford's.

Boots the Chemists, back in the day when they had book and record departments, took a good quantity of my book and put it in their 1982 Christmas catalogue and also asked me to do signings in two shops. The first was in Northampton on a Saturday morning and there was some confusion straight away about where to put me – in the book section or in their slightly smaller record department. As I was now an 'author' I insisted on the book department but it wasn't the most successful book signing debut. I think we managed to sell two copies but the highlight was when a man picked up the hardback book, turned it over a few times and then asked me how much it cost.

To be honest I had to look inside the book jacket to find out that it was £6.95 (it was 1982 and equivalent to almost £23 today). He hesitated for a moment and then asked if it was out in paperback. When I told him that wouldn't be for another few months or so, he simply said, "I'll wait" and walked off.

The next visit was to Portsmouth in the week leading up to Christmas and, after Northampton, I had got all diva-ish and demanded to be in the book department and insisted on photos of the studio around the store. They went along with it and I think they even got some assistants to queue up to get a book signed in order to make me feel good. However, there was one genuine customer who bought a copy of the book and was told by the manager that this was the day when she could have it signed.

The lady came over to my table, I shook her hand, thanked her for buying the book and asked if she wanted it dedicated to anyone. She explained that it was a Christmas present for her son and asked if I would write "To Kevin. Happy Christmas. Love mum xx."

When I had done that, I asked her if she wanted me to sign it and she said "why?" When I told her I had written it, she said "oh, alright then" and so I wrote "And from me too." It seems that she thought I was an in-store Christmas message writing service which went along with gift wrapping. Nothing like a little old lady to put you in your place.

Next, courtesy of my wife, I was now about to become a star of television – at least in East Anglia. Pat went into the local Anglia TV offices in Chelmsford, Essex and told them that her husband (me) had written the history of the world famous Abbey Road studios and that I lived in their region. They said they were interested and we set a date for them to come to the studio with a reporter and a cameraman to film me taking viewers on a tour. All was going well until they decided that they wanted to film me opening the door and walking into the legendary number 2 'Beatles studio'. This meant the cameraman being inside the studio when I entered and him walking backwards as I moved forward. It was then that it all fell apart as he tumbled into a grand piano. The reporter's shout of "cut" was sort of unnecessary to bring things to a temporary halt.

Not being a film or TV star or a famous rock musician, being recognised came as a shock to me the first time it happened, which was in the weeks after the first hardback version of *Abbey Road* was published. On the flyleaf of the book I mentioned that I lived in Great Baddow (a village in Essex) but I didn't expect to be recognized in our local fish and chip shop. There I was buying cod and six penn'orth, when a voice piped up asking if I was Brian Southall. When I admitted that I was, the young man said that he had bought the *Abbey Road* book, read that I was a local and had spent some time looking for me around the village – and now he had caught up with me. He said he wanted me to sign his copy of the book and could he come round to my house to get an autograph. This was not something I was keen on so I suggested we meet the following Friday in the chip shop and he could bring his book with him for me to sign. I was there but he obviously thought it was all a step too far and didn't turn up. That's show business I thought.

There was also the surprise scenario which saw me invited to be a guest speaker at the 1st Mersey Beatle Extravaganza in Liverpool in August 1981, primarily to talk about how we dealt with things at EMI after Lennon's death and any plans we had for future Beatles releases.

The programme for the first Beatles Extravaganza in Liverpool where I was a guest speaker

Of course, I got in a plug for the *Abbey Road* book I was writing. I was on the programme alongside Liverpudlian musician and writer Tony Tyler and novelist and journalist Philip Norman.

I was back there (the Adelphi Hotel in Liverpool) a year later this time with Abbey Road boss Ken Townsend (the book was due in a few months) on a bill that featured local musician Pat Chambers and American Joel Glazier, the man who put forward the "Paul Is Dead" theory following the release of the *Abbey Road* album.

Another moment of 'stardom', in its broadest sense, came a few years later when one of my EMI colleagues excitedly (and with mischievous delight) told me that he had seen my *Abbey Road* book on sale in a nearby Sue Ryder charity shop, marked up at £1.50p. Miffed, I went down to check it out and discovered that the shop was actually on the same spot in Baker Street where The Beatles' Apple boutique had stood two decades earlier. The one saving grace about the incident was that my book - at £1.50p - was still 50p more expensive than the autobiography of 1985 World Snooker champion Dennis Taylor.

Sometime later I appeared in a TV documentary about the Carpenters and this brought me some new fans. My hairdresser told me that she had seen me late at night (a repeat I think) when she was in bed with her partner and when I popped up on the screen she told him, "That's my haircut."

Meanwhile, the local village greengrocer also saw the same show and stopped me in the street to ask if I was who she thought I was and was I in a programme about the Carpenters. I said I was who she thought I was and that I had been in the show. Then, when I went into her shop, she called out to her mate, "It's him off the telly", at which point her colleague shouted back, "And he does his own shopping."

Much less glamorous and much more embarrassing was a man telling me in a public urinal, "Saw you on the telly last night" before walking off. No idea who he was but I think we had gone to the same school many decades earlier.

With around half a dozen titles to my name I became a cruise ship lecturer when I was invited to give talks about my books and life in the music business to passengers on - yes you've guessed it - a Saga cruise for the elderly or senior citizens if you prefer. I have no idea how or why my name got into the frame with the people who booked speakers but there I was being invited, with my wife Pat, on a three week Mediterranean cruise.

The deal is that you only give talks on the days when the ship is at sea, so I was expected to deliver six lectures as we sailed from Southampton to Bordeaux, Bilbao, Porto, Casablanca, Malaga and the Canary Islands before returning to Dover.

I was on the bill with Nicholas Parsons and we shared a table every night for dinner (alongside Mrs Parsons and the husband and wife dance instructors). The lecture hall – which held about 200 – was never packed for my audio visual presentations about all things rock'n'roll, but later, while flicking channels on the ship's in-house TV system, I saw myself lecturing.

Apparently, for those who preferred to stroll the deck, take the sun or sit in the bar rather than listen to me live, they could tune in round the clock and get their dose of musical memories at their own convenience.

Nicholas Parsons did do me the honour of sitting through one of my talks when I told the tale of Pink Floyd's album *Animals* and the flying pig and at the end he took me aside to give me a word of advice. He asked me to confirm that there was a group from the sixties called the Animals and when I said that there was, he suggested that I make it clear that they weren't in the story and that it was about another group because he was a bit confused. Appropriately I took on board what he said but didn't change my act.

A year later I was on another cruise, but this one was just a week long journey into the Norwegian fjords and required only three talks, which meant that the punters didn't get to hear the other three lectures from my repertoire. After that Pat and I decided that cruises were not for us - it was all a bit boring and oddly claustrophobic and, although Saga did a fine job, take my word for it ... once you've seen one fjord you have seen them all.

Mick Hucknall's manager (a man who I knew from East West Records) rang me one day to ask if I would be interested in writing the authorised story of Simply Red who had either just celebrated 21 years together or - by the time it came out – it would be close to their 25th anniversary. Authorised and unauthorised are two words that obviously mean two different things but when it comes to books, a writer has a choice to make. Authorised means working with the subject and having access to all sorts of approved people plus documents and photographs from personal collections. On the downside, the subject has control of the book and can edit or even delete any text they don't like. This can become frustrating for a writer when the person you have written about wants to change something that obviously happened, is almost certainly true and probably in the public domain.

An ex-journalist colleague of mine who wrote some excellent authorised music biographies once told me that one rock star he wrote about wanted all references to his drug-taking removed from his book despite the fact that we all knew, from his own admissions, that he had been treated for heroin addiction. There was also a Jehovah's Witness who, as he did not celebrate birthdays, disputed some parts of the book written about his early life before he became a Witness, claiming that he didn't have a life before joining the religious movement.

On the other hand, unauthorised means the author has a free rein to include anything they find out from their own sources - assuming it is not libellous - but usually do not receive any assistance from the subject or his closest confidantes. I have written both and only once did I get anything more than a polite 'no' after contacting the subject to request their cooperation. A member of a famous rock band actually refused to give me permission to write the book I had planned. His help I would have liked, his permission I did not need.

With Simply Red, Mick Hucknall made himself available for at least three detailed interviews – one in his house, one in Berlin and one in a London hotel – and made sure all people involved with him, including band members, were available to me if they wanted to talk. He gave me a list of names and numbers for family, band members, managers, promoters, record executives, political mate Alastair Campbell, journalists and a football manager – Sir Alex Ferguson – who told me that Hucknall made the right choice with singing as he, "Doesn't have the legs to be a footballer."

At the front of the book, I assembled a bunch of quotes from people who were some of Hucknall's famous friends and fans including (in no particular order) Nelson Mandela, Rt Hon Tony Blair MP, Tom Jones, Rod Stewart, Jools Holland, Van Morrison, David Coulthard, Quincy Jones and Abba's

Frida Lyngstad - but there were a couple of omissions. Actress and ex-girlfriend (Hucknall's not mine) Catherine Zeta Jones didn't make a contribution despite me spending a lot of time trying to make contact - it seems her people couldn't get hold of my people (me) - while getting in touch with film star Jack Nicholson brought a different problem. Hucknall had given me a phone number in California for Nicholson, and assured me he was expecting a call, but it was still with a great deal of trepidation that I rang the great man. The phone was answered by, I think, his Latino housekeeper and a combination of her faltering English and my non-existent Spanish proved a major issue as I tried to explain who I was, why I was calling and ask if Mr Nicholson was available. We got nowhere and although she said she took my name, the man from *The Shining* never called back.

A much easier interviewee was Mick Hucknall's dad Reg in Didsbury near Manchester. Our chat was completed in the house where the singer grew up. A host of early Mancunian contacts also made themselves available. Seemingly less approachable was Simply Red's Japanese guitarist Kenji Suzuki. I had arranged to meet him outside the Hammersmith Odeon and then go for a coffee and a chat. He was someone I had never met before, but I was there at the agreed time and a few minutes later a Japanese man arrived and wandered around outside the hall. I approached him, said "Hi Kenji" and held out my hand. That was when he said "No." Weirdly, it seems that the only two people outside the famous London theatre on that chilly autumn morning were me, waiting for a Japanese man, and a Japanese man who was somebody else. Kenji eventually called to say he was unable to make it, so we arranged another date and all went well. And in the end,

Hucknall didn't change a word of the book although his manager did advise me to alter/drop a couple of things before sending it to the singer for approval.

The whole authorised/non-authorised issue was at the forefront of my plans to write a book about sixties pop group The Hollies. Discussing the idea with a publishing friend, we were astonished to discover that nobody had written a detailed history of the band from Manchester who released over 30 UK hit singles between 1963 and 1993 plus twelve chart albums. They were up there in the premier league alongside their 1960s counterparts The Beatles, Kinks, the Who and the Rolling Stones but were never considered dangerous, exciting or perhaps particularly interesting.

At the outset I tried to make contact with the Hollies manager Jimmy Smith to outline my plan and get the approval of the two 'original' band members still in the band - Tony Hicks and Bobby Elliott. Two phone calls and another two or three emails brought nothing although on one occasion a lady in the office did pick up the phone and tell me that she would get Mr Smith to call me. He didn't, so assuming I was not going to get any help from the band, I ploughed on with the book.

Somewhere along the line I discovered the reason for the non-response ... I was told that Bobby Elliott was going to write the official history of the Hollies. I then offered my services as writer/researcher in that project but that offer was also lost in the ether.

So now it was definitely a case of finding my own way and fortunately I knew enough people who had worked with them over the years to assemble a bunch of fascinating and interesting stories for the book. If Hicks and Elliott weren't coming on board, the band's original bass player Eric Haydock was happy to talk to me in his Stockport home, as was the group's former manager Michael Cohen from his villa in Spain. And, as with all these things, there were two sides to many stories including the one about Haydock's departure from the band.

The man who arguably started it all when he invited two emerging Manchester youngsters Allan Clarke and Graham Nash to join his band the Deltas, told me his version. Haydock said he had some issues over the money the band were earning and demanded Cohen sort it out. "When I got there, Cohen said the boys had had a meeting and decided to let me go." Haydock knew there were stories circulating of him having a girlfriend and being tired with the band's schedule but he denied them. "I didn't leave because of any girlfriend and the nervous exhaustion thing was a press story. The truth was the band sacked me but got Cohen to fire me."

Talking to me on the phone, Cohen explained his version. "The true story about Eric was that he got disillusioned because the band had to go to America and he generally became very difficult. He did miss some gigs and he didn't want to go so we fired him." And then he added, "He never raised any issue about money and he could be surly, moody and miserable."

How two people remember a story or incident is always fascinating and, in previous interviews, both Clarke and Nash have even disagreed on the place where they first ran into their heroes the Everly Brothers in 1960. They agreed that they had seen the duo at Manchester Free Trade Hall and hatched a plan to hang about outside the American duo's hotel and try to catch a glimpse of them. But which hotel was it? Clarke reckons it was the Grand while Nash remembered it as the Midland, but it was a long time ago.

My research included talking to members of other

Manchester groups from the swinging sixties: Peter Noone (Herman's Hermits), The Dreamers (of Freddie and the ... fame) the Dakotas (before Billy J Kramer), and the Fourtones plus songwriters Graham Gouldman and Roger Cook and producer Alan Parsons. Trying to track down and talk to the remaining members of the Hollies proved much more difficult. I struggled to locate Bernie Calvert, Haydock's replacement, as nobody knew where he was and Terry Sylvester - who took over from Graham Nash - said he didn't want to talk as he was saving it all for his own book which, I think, we are all still waiting for.

With Hicks and Elliott out of the picture, that left Clarke and Nash who both appeared on an Abbey Road session form from April 4 1963 which showed that four members of the Hollies were in the studio and were each paid £7. But, for whatever reason, it had Nash listed as a guitarist alongside Haydock, Hicks down as the bass player while Clarke, who was there, doesn't appear at all and Elliott, who wasn't there, was included as a guitarist and somehow even signed for his £7.

Graham Nash corresponded with me by email presumably from his home in Hawaii, and told me what having their first number one hit in July 1965 with 'I'm Alive' meant to the group. "It was a great thrill ... and we realised that having a No.1 song on the radio and TV really meant that we could go to America." As they had been there in April of that year on a Little Richard show in New York, Nash presumably meant "go back to America" which they did in September to tour alongside the Yardbirds.

As for singer Clarke, he told me via email that he had said everything he wanted to say about the Hollies and it was all available on line somewhere. But the man who joined the group in 1961 and left nearly forty years later did confide a couple of things. "I left the Hollies in 1999, have never seen them live since and I don't sing (their songs) in the bath."

So that was that with Hollies I assumed, until a publisher I knew asked me if I would read a book written by one of the Hollies which he had been sent and let him know what I thought. And sure enough it was Bobby Elliott's official story of the group and, sad to say, I reported back that I thought it was "not very exciting." Despite my opinion, the book was published by another publisher and garnered both 5 star and 1 star reviews. We've all been there as authors.

Two other books I look back on with great affection (and a bit of pride even if I do say so myself) came out after we had entered the new millennium. With the help of my great friend and former EMI colleague Rupert Perry, we created the book *Northern Songs* which told the story of how The Beatles lost their songs and their music publishing business. With eight hit singles - all written by John Lennon and Paul McCartney - and four UK number one albums there was a move in 1965 to take the music publishing company Northern Songs, which they had set up with manager Brian Epstein and music publisher Dick James, public. By issuing shares (five million to be exact), the two songwriters would in some way avoid the punitive surtax rate (and they were in that bracket) of 98%. From there the story went on to cover The Beatles failure to acquire the company and their songs, its eventual purchase by Lord Grade (who owned ATV) and the Australian entrepreneur Robert Holmes a' Court who got the songs when he bought ATV parent company ACC (Associated Communications Corporation). It became apparent that he wasn't the nicest or the easiest man to do business with as Lord Grade recounted in his autobiography *Still Dancing*. He wrote, "Robert Holmes a'

Court wasn't the warmhearted Mr. Nice Guy I'd thought he was. He started firing people who were part of the family. He got rid of Katie the tea lady and brought in coffee percolators for the executive offices."

Holmes a' Court's British-born accountant Simon Carrell told me by fax (yes it was that long ago) that his boss simply viewed the ATV company as "a cash cow" before adding, "But it was always in a position of having to perform or be sold." And sell it Holmes a' Court did eventually in 1985 to Michael Jackson for a whopping $47.5 million, ten million more than the starting price as Jackson's lawyer John Branca confirmed. "It might have started at $38 million and then it was $40 million and then $43 million."

Jackson was intent on doing the deal once he had established that neither Lennon's widow Yoko Ono or McCartney had any objection to him buying ATV which included the Northern Songs catalogue. As Holmes a' Court and Jackson finalised the deal, the Australian made two demands. He insisted that Jackson fly to Perth in Western Australia and appear at a Holmes a' Court charity event. One ATV executive, who considered the Australian business man to be a racist and a bigot, told me that Holmes a 'Court wanted the "n***** to dance for him." He also wouldn't sell to Jackson unless the singer gave him one Lennon & McCartney song as a gift for his daughter Catherine. The popular consensus was that he must have wanted 'Yesterday', the most covered song in pop music history, but, it turned out that her favourite was in fact 'Penny Lane' - and to this day she still owns the publishing rights to the 1967 hit.

One final note of absurdity that I discovered writing the story of Northern Songs was that CBS Songs, who administered the ATV catalogue on Jackson's behalf, were intent on acquiring 'Penny Lane' from Catherine Holmes a' Court. However, their efforts were unsuccessful for two reasons - firstly she didn't need the money and secondly CBS executives assumed her name must have been Penny and that was the name they used when sending their best offers to her.

Authors, like musicians and actors, obviously love a good review and tend to ignore the bad ones and, while there were some dissenters about the length and intricacy of the book, there were those on the *Glasgow Evening Times* ("Southall and Perry have done a remarkable job in trying to piece together the puzzle") and *Record Collector* ("industry insiders Southall and Perry do a great job at explaining the story") who were a bit more impressed than the *Dublin Weekend Herald's* opinion that it was "quite a ponderous read" although, on the upside they said, "It has more Beatles photographs." As us writers are always quick to point out, "I didn't write the bloody pictures."

In 2009 I was asked if I would write the story of EMI Records in a book entitled *The Rise And Fall of ...* It felt a little odd as I had spent 15 years at the company, had some very good times and only left because of one particular person who eventually took over at the head of EMI Music. We traced the story from the company's beginning as the Gramophone Company in 1897 through its formation as EMI in 1931, its takeover by Thorn in 1979, the de-merger from Thorn EMI in 1996, its acquisition by Terra Firma in 2007 and - in an updated second edition - its arrival as part of Universal in 2011.

This time-line doesn't include a failed attempt by EMI to merge with the German media giant Bertelsmann (owners of RCA) or unsuccessfully acquire American company Warner Music and, at the time I wrote it, the company was owned by Terra Firma, which was owned by Guy Hands, a man with no history in the music business, who bought it for around £3.2 billion. He was viewed with scepticism, as an outsider and, as Robbie Williams' manager Tim Clark told me, "He is a money man and what he deals with is figures, and if the figures ain't working he'll get out." Chris Hufford, co-manager of EMI acts Radiohead and Supergrass, was similarly wary, saying "He's a bright man but has absolutely no idea about the music business" while Chris Morrison, who looked after Blur and Gorillaz, added, "I have no idea what was behind Hands buying EMI."

One of the weirdest things was when I interviewed Hands on the telephone. It had been arranged by his PR man but, after the conversation, he came on the phone to tell me that I couldn't use anything Hands had told me as a direct quote which took me by surprise. I protested, pointing out that previous senior executives Colin Southgate, Jim Fifield and Eric Nicoli had all spoken to me both candidly and on the record. In the end I reluctantly agreed although some of what he said did appear in the book as direct quotes attributed to an EMI "spokesperson" or "senior executive." Those readers who spotted his quotes could have won a coconut or an EMI contract.

Prior to Hands and Terra Firma, EMI boss, Southgate hired Jim Fifield, an American, to head up EMI Music Worldwide and purge the company of its old guard - including yours truly. In order to create what he called a "winning culture," he pronounced that "constructive conflict is far more productive than passive agreement."

Things can change dramatically and quickly in business and sure enough when it came time for Southgate to go, Fifield saw himself as the obvious successor BUT some didn't agree. As Southgate said, "I was due to retire and he

(Fifield) wanted to become chairman (of the EMI company) but the board didn't want him as chairman. He started to play politics - it was nothing to do with him being American."

For his part in it all, Fifield told me he had no problem with Southgate being chairman (of the EMI company) but that he did have "a major problem with him (Southgate) wanting to run it (EMI Music)." He told me, "Colin would push and I would push back and eventually it unwound itself." So that chapter ended in tears and then the whole thing tumbled into a pantomime which was best described by a former EMI colleague. When I told him I was going to write the book covering EMI's fall from grace and its future prospects, he just said, "What a shit show that is."

Among other titles I have written over the years are books about The Beatles, Bob Dylan, the Bee Gees, Pink Floyd, Sex Pistols, 1950s rock'n'roll, and Jimi Hendrix which involved me talking to Queen guitarist Brian May who was a huge fan of the guitarist and, while on the entertainment committee at Imperial College London, had booked Hendrix and the Experience to appear for £1000. May told me that there was one thing about Hendrix's appearance that struck a chord with him. "I had spent a long time feeling embarrassed about the way I looked because I had curly hair and it was very uncool to have curly hair in the mid-60s." But then things changed. "Suddenly I saw Hendrix and he had curly hair and he was proud of it and that liberated me. I thought it's alright, I don't have to iron my hair flat anymore. I'd been straightening it for years using an iron. I went to endless lengths to not have curly hair and then suddenly because of Hendrix it was cool."

In addition to anniversary books about *Sgt Pepper* and *The White Album*, I wrote *The Beatles Album By Album* when I asked musicians, producers, disc jockeys, composers, journalists and friends to talk about their favourite Beatles album. And the winner was *Please Please Me* with five people – including me – selecting it as not necessarily the best but the most influential album by the band. *Sgt Pepper* was next with three votes.

The book I wrote for the 50th anniversary of the album *Sgt Pepper* earned me a trip to New York where in just three days I did more interviews than the average politician during an election campaign. The American publishers flew me out (courtesy of budget airline Norwegian) and put me in a reasonable 3 star hotel near Madison Square Garden, which was a step down from the luxury Plaza, Four Seasons, Riga, Meridian, St Regis and Mandarin hotels where I ended up on record company expenses.

In just one day, one of the hottest May days on record in New York when temperatures soared to 33 centigrade, I did 20 radio interviews between 9 am and 12 noon with stations calling in from all over the USA. The next day there were a further six phone interviews with newspapers from Connecticut to New Jersey plus a taped appearance for NBC TV and an early morning live interview on Fox TV's *Good Day New York*.

It was a hectic but fun few days, marred only by a driver deliberately crashing his car in Times Square killing one person and injuring 20 more, and I got more publicity for one book in just three days than for all my other books put together. And among the reviews was one from the prestigious *Wall St Journal* which wrote, "Mr. Southall's book will be a handy primer for children and aide-mémoire for boomers who have entered senescence without ever leaving their adolescence." I couldn't have put it better myself and so polite.

This manic three day promo tour in America compared incredibly unfavourably with the efforts of my English publisher Carlton (since taken over and re-named) who managed to get me a total of ZERO interviews with UK media although I did arrange to give a talk in my local library which turned out to be the highlight. Actually, it sat alongside another stand-out moment as, sometime after visiting the US, I received a copy of an audio tape of my *Sgt. Pepper* book read by a man called Johnny Haller who, it says on the sleeve notes, is a multiple Earphones Awards winner and been named among the Top 50 Narrators by *Audio File*. Looking at it now, it reminds me I must listen to it sometime.

Just to be fair to our country's media outlets - both printed and broadcast - I have done a fair share of interviews over the years for the various books I have been lucky enough to have published - some arranged by Carlton - and they have included radio slots with the likes of Janice Long, Cerys Matthews, Vanessa Feltz, Keith Skues, Spencer Leigh and Robert Elms not forgetting the prestigious *Today* programme or my local BBC Essex station, who have had me on more times than is probably good for the average listener.

Chapter 15

WITH MY PR HAT ON ...

"Out of adversity comes opportunity," said Benjamin Franklin, one of America's founding fathers, back in the 18th century. Two centuries on it was a phrase that came to apply to me and my career at EMI and it arrived directly from the 'adversity' of us signing the Sex Pistols.

After what was considered to be something of a PR disaster for the company as the Corporation's executives briefed their spokespeople in an attempt to placate all areas of the media, the man who followed Leslie Hill into the seat as MD of EMI Records was a true Spanish gentleman. Ramon Lopez was an International director for the company before taking charge of an operation that was feeling its way back into the music business. He approached me with an offer to return to a PR role as the UK Record division's first official Communications Manager - I hung out for the title Director but didn't get it.

Lopez was of the view that EMI Records should make its own decisions, policies and statements when it came to its acts thus avoiding the potential embarrassment of Corporate poking their nose in. My new role was a slightly weird one as there had never been a PR man for the record company and it was an eye-opener to sit in on management meetings and find out what was going on at a level that had previously been way above my pay grade. For instance I found out that our finance director, James Tyrell, who also held the post of Head of the HMV chain of record shops (which we owned), actually had to write to himself when it came to EMI changing their terms of trading with retailers. And, in line with his retail colleagues, he replied to himself to disagree. Eventually, however, HMV Tyrell had to give in to EMI Tyrell and the new terms were introduced.

Trading terms in Japan were on the agenda when a collection (is there another collective noun – maybe an album or release) of record retailers from that part of the world arrived in the UK to discuss the impact of retail price maintenance being removed. This had already happened in the UK which meant that retailers were free to sell records at whatever price they liked – hence the arrival of discounting and price wars. When around 20 dealers from Japan arrived (courtesy of our Japanese company), I was given the task of arranging for them to meet people from major record stores HMV, Our Price and Harlequin, to explain through an interpreter (which meant it took ages) the pros and cons and ups and downs of retail price maintenance disappearing. That done, I was then left to find something for them to do on their night off. It came to me in a flash - the ballet. They must have them in Japan I thought, there's no language barrier and there's music in it. So in mid-afternoon, through the one interpreter, I sent them on their way from the Dominion Theatre in Tottenham Court Road, where the London Ballet Company were performing, with strict instructions to be back there by 6.30pm. Now I had no idea about Japanese businessmen abroad and what they might get up to when free to roam the streets of Soho. I don't think any of them actually visited any professional ladies who advertised in Wardour, Greek, Dean, Berwick or Old Compton Streets ("French lessons 2nd Floor" / "Big Chest for sale 1st floor") but they did have a grand time buying some very iffy accessories and equipment which, and this was a big surprise, they flaunted around the theatre lobby. These were their special souvenirs of London - which buzzed and whirred - and I assume they went home happy. I have to admit that Soho was probably more fun than the ballet.

After the Pistols adventure, it was obvious EMI needed to improve its image and reputation - hence my appointment as Communications Manager. It had even become the butt of a music industry joke which ran as follows: "What's the difference between EMI and the Titanic? At least the Titanic had a good band." Boom boom. This one ran alongside a joke about the other major British record company: "My son asked for a cowboy outfit for Christmas so I bought him Decca."

Both organisations survived these one-liners and when we at EMI were officially listed as the top company for singles and albums in 1976, 1977 and 1978 we came back with a badge - and this was very much the era of lapel badges - which showed the Titanic as a high speed motor boat belting through the sea with the tagline "You can't keep a good ship down." That told 'em we thought.

In 1980 we were approached by the BBC to take part in a reality TV show called *The Big Time* which would show how a new young artist might get a recording contract - if they were good enough. The programme's host, Esther Rantzen, had chosen a 21-year-old Scottish singer named Sheena Easton to be the subject and I was required to act as some sort of liaison officer between the BBC crew and EMI - a meeting of two giant corporations. We gave them the small Manchester Square studio to shoot in and did our best to be helpful whilst keeping a low profile as we weren't convinced that it was the sort of contrived 'talent show' that we should be involved with.

Rantzen was, I recall, a bit shouty and quite demanding of her team while our A&R people hung around in the background without committing to any sort of a deal. However, by the time the show was aired in August, the powers-that-be had decided to offer Sheena Easton a contract.

I'm not sure who chose her manager - her or us - but she linked up with former EMI fifties singer Deke Arlon (whose wife Jill played Josephina in the TV soap *Crossroads*). who also managed Dennis Waterman - who was then signed to EMI. Sheena Easton then went out on tour in 1980 with Waterman, who was signed to EMI and also managed by Arlon. I went to see them in Glasgow and bought yet another dinner.

As they often say, the rest is history. Easton went on to a major international hit-making career, selling over 40 million records worldwide, so maybe the BBC were right to choose her back then.

My abiding memory of Waterman is of us agreeing to allow EMI's Manchester Square to be used for filming an episode of *Minder* the TV series he starred in alongside George Cole. We received some sort of fee for making our offices available and I got to not only meet Cole - a hero from the *St Trinian's* films of the fifties and sixties - but also pocket a signed copy of a *Minder* script.

Abbey Road, even before I wrote the book about its history, was on my beat as head of PR for EMI UK which oversaw the north London studio. This involved me working with its general manager Ken Townsend, a man who started there in 1954 and progressed through the ranks. He was devoted to the studio and its history while welcoming new equipment and recording techniques alongside new artists.

In 1980 there was a decision made to hold an auction in the studio - advertised as a music industry event not open to the public - to sell off redundant equipment and a few mementoes from its history. The cavernous Studio One - usually reserved for classical works - was packed with all sorts of items including mixing consoles, loudhailers, microphones and, most exciting of all, equipment used by The Beatles.

A Studer J37 four track recorder used on *Sgt Pepper* went for £500 while Mike Oldfield (he of *Tubular Bells* fame) bought a Mellotron tape organ plus original tapes used by the 'fab four' for £1,000. A copy of Brian Epstein's book *A Cellarful of Noise*, signed by The Beatles and producer George Martin, went for £210 while something dubbed "Ringo Starr's ashtray" fetched £135. The ashtray was at the top of a brass stand and stood about 75cm (2'6") tall and it had a regular place next to Ringo's drum kit during their sessions, even appearing in some photographs. But what the woman who bought in the auction might not have known was that it actually dated back to the 1930s and over the years it had been used by a host of drummers and pianists including Mrs Mills, a London born pianist who hit the singles chart in 1961.

Ken Townsend told me that when Mrs Mills went into hospital during the 1960s, the ashtray was delivered to her bedside - those were the days when you could have a fag in your hospital bed - and she returned it to the studio when she recovered. Some years after the auction, the woman who bought the ashtray contacted Townsend, who had also bid for it in the original sale, and offered to sell it to him at the price she paid. On one of my visits to his home, he brought it out to show it off.

Arriving a year too late to make use of the famous ashtray was West Germany's Chancellor Helmut Schmidt. It's not often that a major politician arrives in a recording studio to actually make a record but Schmidt was one of the few. He turned up at Abbey Road in 1981 to record Mozart's *Piano Concertos* for our classical division and I was on corporate patrol to meet and greet and wave the flag. When I arrived, traffic was at a standstill in St John's Wood and I even spotted an armed officer or two around the studio. As I got to the front door I suddenly became conscious of the fact that I was wearing a knee length 'SS style' leather coat which might not have gone down well, so just to be on the safe side, I dumped it at reception before going into studio 1. Herr Schmidt was charming and happily posed for a few photographs although he insisted that none were taken while he was smoking. He somehow assumed his wife didn't know he smoked although it seemed that the rest of the world did.

Three years after the auction, Abbey Road threw open its doors to the public for the first time in its, by then 50 year history, as the control room in Studio Two was being refurbished and updated. In order to do this there were serious conversations - and agreements reached - with the local council and residents' associations who anticipated coachloads of noisy and disruptive fans during the three months from July to September when the officially titled The Beatles At Abbey Road Studios Presentation ran for seven days a week. For £4.50 visitors got a tour of the studio complex before refreshments were served - soft drinks and cakes - and then came the main event; a 90-minute presentation shown in Studio Two featuring rare film clips, promotional videos and even some previously unreleased Beatles recordings. The big concern we all had were bootleggers who we knew would relish the opportunity to tape the show and even release it as a bootleg.

Despite signs saying "No Sound recordings may be made of this presentation", some were not put off and, after one fan was caught trying to tape the show, metal detectors were installed in the entrance. But, despite everybody's best efforts, a copy was made - and subsequently released in America - by collectors who took apart a cassette player/recorder and stuffed the parts into various bags under some of the souvenirs on sale at the studio.

There was even talk at one time of Abbey Road becoming home to some sort of rock'n'roll exhibition but the burghers of St John's Wood were never going to go along with that idea - three Beatles shows a day for three months was as much as they were prepared to put up with. But, to this day, the fans still come to disrupt the traffic by walking across, and posing on, the zebra crossing in the face of oncoming cars and buses.

With the departure of Ramon Lopez, followed quickly by both John Bush and Cliff Busby (who eventually left after an unfortunate drink driving incident), Peter Jamieson arrived from EMI Australia in 1982 to take over as head of EMI Records UK.

Then, for reasons best known to himself, he made me head of radio and TV promotion while also looking after the company's PR needs.

At that time I knew very few people in radio and TV and soon realised that the pluggers who worked for me were intent on keeping their contacts as far away from me as possible. Theirs was a closed network of producers and presenters and I was only invited in when there was an irate manager moaning about lack of airplay and demanding we hire (and pay for) an independent plugger.

It was always interesting to note that when a record one of my people took round to radio was turned down as not 'good enough', a manager's solution was to get somebody else to take the same record into the same people in the hope that they would change their mind. Funnily enough it rarely worked like that. The great producer Mickie Most, whose records on RAK we worked, was a man who never moaned about a rejection or thought about editing a record to change it. He simply said, "I'll have to make another one."

As we also worked on records from artists signed to Capitol and EMI America, there were often heated conversations with their managers who really failed to grasp how radio in the UK worked compared with the US. While there was no national music station in America, each major city had around ten stations playing rock and pop music so getting a handsome 15 plays a week on BBC Radio1, alongside maybe a dozen on the commercial stations around the country, was considered by them to be small beer. It was a scenario which the manager of Bob Seger, who told me that his artist would "go platinum in Detroit" and pick up hundreds of plays around the states, never really understood.

Explaining how British music radio worked to American managers and artists was up there alongside giving lessons in cricket.

While Seger only toured the UK once, which didn't help his cause, there were other American acts who showed up on our radar including Dr Hook, Heart and Tina Turner who came to the company with the acquisition of United Artists. Having left Ike Turner, she embarked on a solo career which brought her into regular contact with my promotion team as she toured the UK and made a host of TV and radio appearances.

Less helpful than the late Tina Turner who happily did her bit with the media, was America's leading underground musician Frank Zappa who came to us in the UK via a strange deal with his Barking Pumpkin label. In all honesty I can't even remember which records we released although two albums from that early eighties period – *Ship Arriving Too Late To Save A Drowning Man* and *The Man From Utopia* – were minor UK hits. It was with some foreboding that I agreed to join my colleague David Munns for a dinner with Zappa at Julie's, an industry hang-out in Shepherd's Bush.

It wasn't a warm and cuddly evening as Zappa was a little off with us from the outset. I sensed that in his 15 year career he had met with, and fallen out with, a whole bunch of record company execs – and we were not going to be the exceptions.

I have no idea what was on the agenda – a release, a tour, promo opportunities – but I remember getting the sharp end of his tongue when I asked about his children Dweezil and Moon Unit. I had the temerity to refer to his daughter simply as 'Moon' and he quickly chastised me, saying that her name is Moon Unit ... maybe she's known as Moon only by family and close friends. It turned out that Zappa is also very fussy about wine – red in particular. Whether he is a connoisseur or just an awkward bugger, either way he rejected at least six different bottles of red – which we gratefully finished (we were paying after all) – until something struck the right note and then he ordered quite a lot of them.

As part of my new role, I flew out to America with the new marketing head David Hughes, who had worked with me at *Disc* a decade earlier before joining Polydor and then

EMI. We were there to introduce ourselves to the people at Capitol and EMI America and as part of that exercise we attended marketing and promotion meetings where they spoke a different language.

There were conversations about primary, secondary and "thirdary" radio stations – what happened to tertiary we wondered – and even "garment feasibility" which was a question about whether or not to make a t-shirt to go with the album.

However, my abiding memory is of taking David Hughes to Los Angeles airport (he was flying back before me) and driving through Watts as the petrol gauge got closer and closer to empty. At that time Watts, a bit like Harlem in New York, was not the safest place for two white boys to be seen in and, as the designated driver, I told Hughes that if we did run out of petrol, he was doing the pushing. With a bit of luck and some careful management of our limited resources by me, we made it to a 'safe' gas station and to the airport on time.

During 1982 there was a major lunch thrown at one of the posh Mayfair hotels to celebrate what must have been the 15th anniversary of BBC Radio 1 and, as head of radio and TV promotion, I was there. I can't recall whether it was an EMI 'do' or an industry-wide event, but it sticks in my mind as it was the one and only time I came across Jimmy Savile.

The entire entertainment industry had heard all sorts of rumours and horror stories about the man and indeed I was always reluctant to take my daughter to any *Jim'll Fix It* shows (although she did get to go to *Crackerjack* and *Saturday Superstore*) for fear she might be picked out by Saville.

But, despite what a lot of people in television, radio and the music business were aware of, neither the BBC nor various police forces carried out any rigorous reviews into his behaviour.

But here he was, in the flesh - in a gold tracksuit, with sunglasses and the usual prop cigar - and even then he had to hog all the limelight and make a spectacle of himself by arriving after all his colleagues from Radio 1 (presenters, producers and executives) and, instead of acknowledging any of the guests, he made straight for the waitresses and serving ladies and made sure they all got a kiss or a hug or an autograph.

It was ugly to watch but every one of those women went home convinced he was a warm and cuddly human being until they, like the rest of us, read the headlines and heard the allegations which began appearing in the 1990s.

In my role as the company's head of corporate PR, I dealt with a multitude of requests for support and sponsorship for school fetes, sports events (and teams) and charity fundraisers but one request did catch my eye. It came from a British mountaineering team who wanted some music to take up the mountain with them.

The six person team (five men and one woman) were going to tackle the world's 14th highest peak - the 26,398ft Xixabangma (or Shisha Pangma) - in the Himalayas and their request resonated with me as I thought back to the company's support for other explorers in days of yore. Back in 1910 the Gramophone Company had loaned a gramophone and 100 78 rpm shellac discs (mainly Clara Butt and Enrico Caruso) to Robert Scott's ill-fated expedition to the South Pole.

While none of Scott's team of five survived, somehow the gramophone found its way back to the UK and remains in the company archive.

Nearly two decades later, the company gave another

gramophone (plus discs of the day) to a combined British/Australian/New Zealand team for their trip to the Antarctic. Now, nigh on 50 years later, I had the chance to support another team of brave Brits (I assumed they were all British) as they made their way, in May 1982, up a very, very tall mountain. And all they wanted from me were some cassettes to liven up their journey through Nepal.

A postcard from a Tibetan mountain where a team of climbers (hopefully) enjoyed some EMI Music in their tent

I can't remember exactly what I sent them but the package would probably have included the latest releases from Cliff Richard, the Rolling Stones, Paul McCartney and Queen alongside Olivia Newton-John, Diana Ross and Iron Maiden. In return I got a postcard signed by the team - sent from China with local stamps featuring mushrooms - which said; "Going up to base camp tomorrow. Many thanks for your tapes. Regards." Did they bring them back or did they leave them up there to be enjoyed by those who followed in their footsteps ... we'll never know.

My new boss Peter Jamieson, unlike Ramon Lopez, was all in favour of a bit of personal publicity and he was delighted when I got him on Gloria Hunniford's Radio Two afternoon show to talk about how record companies (mainly EMI) operated. He even gave me a name check and described me as being "ubiquitous" which I think was a compliment. His next appearance was on BBC TV's *Saturday Superstore* with Sarah Green and Mike Read where he once again talked about how the record business worked and even took questions from some interested children. We sat back and bathed in the glory that he was quite possibly the first MD of a record company to do these shows.

But not everything ran in Jamieson's favour as an investigation in 1984 into EMI breaking the UK's official chart code loomed on the horizon. The official chart compilers Gallup were looking into accusations that the EMI sales force had broken the rules by offering boxes of 25 Queen albums to promote a single by the band Re-flex. It was OK to give away free records from an act but they couldn't be used to promote a record by a different artist. While neither Re-flex nor Queen would have been aware of what was going on, somebody within EMI probably was, but nobody was going to be hung out to dry even if they had deliberately broken the rules. In a statement that I almost certainly wrote, Jamieson explained, "Unfortunately, being unaccustomed to giving away free product, a number of our sales reps directly related free product to the week's sales and promotion effort on sales. This gave rise to a technical breach of the chart's code of conduct."

So that was our excuse - over-enthusiastic sales reps not understanding the rules. The British Phonographic Industry (BPI), following the investigation, then had to give out their official view of the situation. In a statement which I helped write, they explained, "No evidence whatsoever was provided that any dealers had made false entries in Dataport Retailers (for singles sales) or had been asked to do so by any EMI rep." If the single involved was Re-flex's 'The Politics of Dancing', then whatever the EMI reps did or didn't do wasn't very effective as the record stiffed at No. 28.

If that scenario wasn't exactly breaking the rules, there was another more expensive way for us to promote a new band and this involved getting them the support spot on a tour by a major selling artist. The downside for us was that it usually cost thousands of pounds to do so. A promoter, or even a manager, might come up with the idea of putting on a new act to open for the top of the bill but nothing was for free. The idea was that we, EMI, would throw in £10k or even £15k to help put the show on the road and in return one of our up-and-coming artists would get a 20 minute spot before the interval.

Kate Bush was rightly suspicious of this when she turned down the support spot on Fleetwood Mac's *Rumours* tour of the US, but some managers liked the idea of their act having a few minutes in the spotlight, albeit usually before the interval. The other down side for them was that as the support act they rarely got a proper sound check and often ended up playing to a half-full hall as fans of the headliners stayed in the bar or were still parking their cars.

I'm still not sure how I got involved in the plan to create a weekend of music programmes to be broadcast on cable solely for the people of Swindon for nothing - whether they liked it or not. The original Thorn company had bought Radio Rentals in 1968 and that, somehow or other, gave them a stake in cable television in the Wiltshire city through the business of renting radios, televisions and video players and, according to the Thorn EMI annual report of 1983, the company's "initial intention is to expand in Swindon and our other existing areas of cable operation."

This led to four of us – under the auspices of EMI Records music video arm – setting to work on creating *Music Box* as the first cable music channel in the country in 1984. I was joined by No.1 record producer (Pilot and Steve Harley) and million-selling artist Alan Parsons, TV presenter Steve Blacknell and EMI colleague Alison Lewis. As the author of the *Abbey Road* book, I was now in addition to my day job, viewed as the company's wordsmith and was called on to write advertising supplements, sleeve notes and conference speeches.

With *Music Box* I scripted various shows and even hosted some as we featured Thin Lizzy, Flock of Seagulls, Lemmy from Motorhead and a chat show with Duran Duran's John Taylor and Queen's Roger Taylor plus Kim Wilde. And, obviously, there had to be a feature on Abbey Road, which I wrote and narrated while Parsons directed the camera inside and outside where I became a roving reporter and almost died for my art, thanks to the man who worked on The Beatles Saville Row live performance. He had me walk towards him on the edge of the pavement talking into a microphone prior to going across the famous crossing BUT what he didn't tell me was that at one stage a huge lorry was coming up behind me which, while it didn't hit me, did blow me off my stroke. And it was greeted with howls of laughter by the three man crew.

To put all this material together - with a bunch of music videos - required the four of us to spend at least two nights in Swindon, famous as the birthplace of actress Diana Dors (originally Fluck), singer Billie Piper, Supertramp's Rick Davies and the band XTC. As this was before we opened EMI's CD factory in the town, we were all strangers in a strange land even though it did have cable TV. What they made of us back then we never found out but our masters at Thorn EMI were seemingly not overly impressed as they moved Music Box into Richard Branson's Virgin empire and the whole thing closed down in 1987.

Way back in 1975 we signed Ray Jackson, a singer from the Newcastle group Lindisfarne, to a contract which committed us to release three singles in the first year. For reasons unknown to me - maybe because it wasn't a hit - we only issued one, 'Take Some Time', which resulted in Jackson and his manager suing us for failing to promote his single properly and for not issuing the other two records. Our argument, as I recall, was that the music Jackson was delivering "was not satisfactory and would have been a commercial failure".

Over a ten year period I presume lawyers on both sides continued the argument until the case came to court in Newcastle in March 1985 and I, together with a marketing executive witness and our legal eagle, trooped up to the north east to sit through the trial which did not go our way. The judge ruled that according to the contract, Jackson was not obliged to provide his own material and Jackson and his manager were awarded damages and costs against the company to a total of £23,304. I'm not sure if this set any sort of a precedent but certainly the Backstreet Boys and Michael Jackson both sued their record labels in the early 2000s for not giving the proper support or promotion to their releases - but it was a first time for us ... and we had a whole host of artists whose records hadn't struck gold. But it's probably (and hopefully) too late now for them to take us to court.

Although we fell out with Ray Jackson, there were other, perhaps more distinguished, artists with long EMI careers who we celebrated generously. Opera singer Elizabeth Schwarzkopf signed to EMI in 1946 and in 1986 she joined us at Manchester Square for lunch to celebrate 40 years with the company. For some reason the head of corporate PR (me), who had never met her, was among the dozen or so guests around the table in the EMI boardroom. She was regal and wonderfully diva-ish as she spoke about her career, although she skipped over the famous moment in 1958 when she chose seven of her own recordings for the radio programme *Desert Island Discs*. She explained to the producers, "I will stick to my own records."

Organist Reginald Dixon was probably the longest serving EMI act when we celebrated his 50 years with a luncheon in 1982 - he had signed to Zonophone in 1932, the year after EMI was founded. We dined in the nearby Durrants Hotel, an establishment with a history of accommodating doctors from the nearby Harley and Wigmore Streets. Again he was an artist I had never met but as PR chief I was there to fly a flag - but not pay the bill - and my abiding memory is of a waiter who had a very shaky serving arm (nowadays probably diagnosed as Parkinson' Disease) which meant when he asked "peas sir?", you got some whatever you said. Years later, Victoria Wood's soup sketch with Julie Walters as the 'shaky' waitress brought it all back to me.

Another event I attended with my PR badge on my lapel was the *This Is Your Life* TV programme for Joe Loss in 1990, when he celebrated 50 years in show business. I had never been to a recording of this show before, but it involved guests arriving at the Portman Hotel in Portman Square for tea and cakes about four hours before the show started.

Among the guests were Lionel Blair and his sister Joyce, Vera Lynn, Spike Milligan, Jon Pertwee and singer Ross McManus, with his son Elvis Costello. None of them were on my table, as I sat with sixties pop idol Jess Conrad. We made conversation, talked about his hits and film parts but neither of us ever mentioned his record 'This Pullover' which, in 1977, had been voted The World's Worst Record on Kenny Everett's Capital Radio Show. I could have reassured him by saying that I hadn't voted for it … without telling him that I lived outside London and couldn't get Capital Radio.

The compact disc arrived in around 1982 and as the joint Sony Philips technology gathered steam (or laser power) the record companies had to consider this new format to go alongside records and cassettes, having disposed of 8-tracks years earlier. Some companies were quicker off the mark than EMI as we were reluctant to commit to a change that might have cost us a lot of money.

As the technology was Japanese/Dutch, we would have had to pay the two companies a royalty to manufacture whatever we decided to release. My quote as the corporate mouthpiece went along these lines; "The question of the royalty (to Sony & Philips) will have to be discussed should we decide to manufacture our own CD product." This didn't go down well with some of our best-selling artists who were keen to see their titles out on the latest format, particularly when Dire Straits topped the million sales mark with their CD version of *Brothers in Arms* in 1985.

Bands like The Beatles, Pink Floyd and Queen were eager to be involved and, sure enough, in 1986 we opened our first compact disc manufacturing plant in Swindon where Thorn, who had bought EMI for £165 million in 1979, had some operations. Through the good offices of local MP Simon Coombes, we got John Butcher, Under Secretary at the Board of Trade, to open the site and the first title off the production line was Pink Floyd's *Dark Side of The Moon*. Even then there were significant rows with artists and managers about the royalties EMI paid on their CD sales as we claimed that a lower royalty rate reflected the significant R&D (research & development) costs involved in setting up the new facility. Obviously that only worked for a few months before re-negotiations took place and new royalties on CD sales were put in place.

We did manage to sort things out by 1987 in order to release The Beatles' *Sgt Pepper* album on its 20th anniversary with the tagline: "It was 20 years ago today," thanks to Lennon and McCartney.

If there were differences regarding CD releases, there were bigger issues in South Africa as major decisions opposing the country's apartheid regime were being taken on the international stage. America declared sanctions and members of the Commonwealth agreed a series of economic sanctions, while UK Prime Minister Margaret Thatcher only agreed to "voluntary" bans on tourism and investment in the country.

As EMI had a record company and factory in Johannesburg, there were concerns about Thorn EMI's position, and for some reason I was sent to Johannesburg in 1986 to meet with management and union officials to assure them that we were not pulling out or reducing our investment in the company. The whole trip was an eye-opener which began with seeing EMI's leading South African artist Johnny Clegg, an anti-apartheid activist whose nickname was "the white Zulu", appear in concert in my hotel. He was an exciting, energetic and dedicated performer who thrilled a multi-racial audience.

The next day I visited the factory where, echoing the words of the Thorn EMI board, I told them that it was "business as usual". That was when I learned that some sections of a militant anti-apartheid movement had taken to sabotaging the record factory by pouring sawdust or sand into the vinyl presses. This was explained to me as part of a plan to get the British parent company to pull out of South Africa. However, neither Thatcher nor Thorn EMI were set to give up and the company rolled on.

That trip, in addition to having to get a special passport and visa so that I didn't get a South African stamp in my regular passport, also brought me close (perhaps too close) to the violence that was regularly reported in the UK press. While the black segregated township of Soweto was closed to all visitors while I was there due to outbreaks of violence, you could visit the township of Alexandra, which was established in 1912.

I went there with the head of EMI South Africa - a Boer with, it has to be said, slightly racist tendencies - and as we pulled up at a set of traffic lights in his company Mercedes, he looked over and asked if the doors were locked and the windows closed. I told him they were and asked why. That was when he explained, in his own terms, that when fancy cars with white people in them stopped at junctions or lights in townships, some locals might pull open a door or put a hand through an open window while clutching a hand grenade. The pin would still be in but they were ready to pull it if you didn't get out and hand over the car.

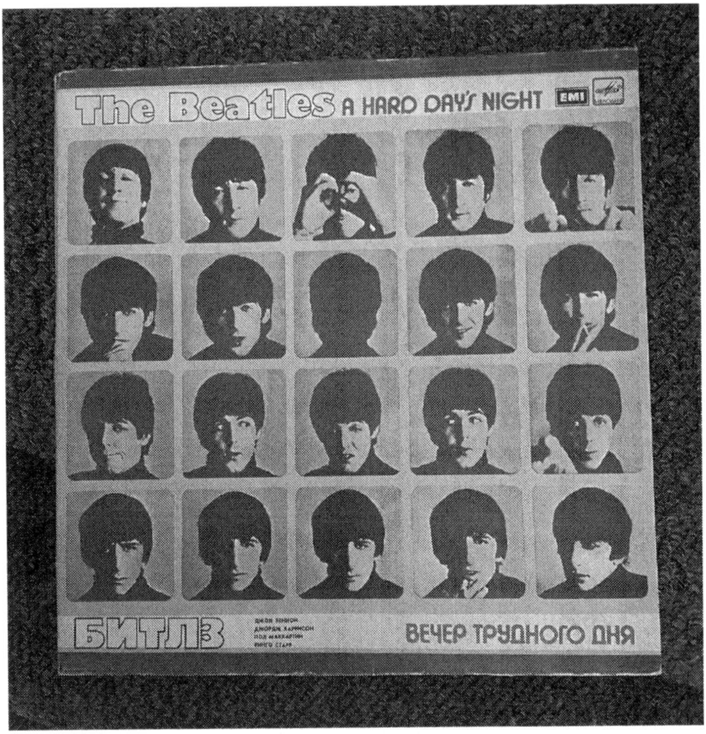

Back In The USSR - the first Beatles album issued in the Soviet Union

Other overseas countries provided less volatile, but more practical problems. A year before The Beatles came out on CD, their recordings did appear officially in the USSR for the first time when we did a deal with the local state owned Melodiya record company. The album was called *A Hard Day's Night* but was a double album made up of 28 tracks taken from the band's first four albums and under the deal, negotiated with approval from Apple, Melodiya paid an agreed royalty based on the production and sale of, I think something like 100,000 records. It might have been more but I remember asking, as I created a press release, who kept a check on how many were actually manufactured or sold? There didn't seem to be an answer and although we did receive the agreed monies there was no guarantee that we - and The Beatles - shouldn't have got a few bob (or roubles) more.

As EMI had a presence in Mexico, courtesy of Bhaskar Menon, the head of EMI Music and my boss, I managed to get an all-expenses paid trip there to see the 1986 World Cup Final between Argentina and West Germany (as it still was then) and all I had to do was promise to bring him back a couple of programmes for his sons. Weirdly, EMI Music had no travel department or official travel agency so we were all free to use whoever we liked to book flights and hotels and the invoices were sent through to the company for payment. The man who ran the company I used was somebody who I had known for years and, when he booked flights for me to travel to Los Angeles, he came up with the plan that if I could get to Mexico City on Sunday June 19, he and his partner would meet me with a ticket for the final.

I had never visited the EMI company in Mexico before, which was run back then by an Englishman (we were all over the place running companies in those days) and Menon thought it would be a good idea for me to pay a visit – on his one condition.

The match kicked off at noon in the midday sun and, ever watchful, no drinks with ice in them were bought at the game for fear of food (or drink) poisoning.

We all know now that the match ended with Argentina

(with Maradona) winning, but in the stands where we sat there was another tussle going on between sets of supporters of the two teams who were shouting and throwing plastic cups at each other. The partner in the travel company, a large imposing figure, was in the mood to confront them all and tell them to behave. It was then that I, or my travel man, reminded him that we were three Englishman sitting in between football fans from two countries that we had 'history' with ... in 1914-18, 1939-45 (Germany) and in 1982 the Falklands War (Argentina). He sat down and kept quiet while I concentrated on getting my three football programmes.

There is no real history of British royalty visiting any of EMI's operations in the UK, although a couple of Prime Ministers (Winston Churchill - before my time - and Margaret Thatcher - after I had left) had called in at Abbey Road Studios which had recorded and broadcast, via land lines from BBC Studios, Christmas messages by reigning monarchs, and the coronations of King George VI and Queen Elizabeth II.

However, in October 1986 we got a call from our company in Thailand to say that Her Royal Highness Princess Chulabhorn, the youngest daughter of the King of Thailand, was visiting the UK and wanted to go to Abbey Road Studios. She had made albums in her homeland with our company with proceeds from her sales going to hospitals and medical research. Preparations for the royal visit involved me going to the Thai Embassy in Queen's Gate for a meeting with a high-ranking official who invited me to join him for tea as we discussed arrangements - and that was when I got my first surprise.

When the lady carrying the tea and cups on a tray entered the room, she dropped to her knees and shuffled her way to a table before leaving the same way. It seems that in Thai society bosses are superior to subordinates and this meant she was 'below' the Embassy official but probably not me.

I saw this hierarchical system in action again at Abbey Road where the Princess sat in a low chair and when the Ambassador (or similar) came across to speak with her, he was quite literally on the floor in keeping with the custom of being 'below' the Royal Family. It was very odd particularly as the Abbey Road staff were able to stand and talk to her about the studio.

After the visit, Princess Chulabhorn, whose brother is now the King of Thailand, came to our offices in Gloucester Place for a formal meet and greet. We all stood in a line and she came along the line, shook hands with us and gave each of us a gift. In her homeland, in accordance with the Royal family's divine status, she would not have shaken hands with the likes of us but the Embassy staff told us that she would make an exception to greet us as 'westerners'. We were each given a couple of books about her country - in the Thai language - and also a Thai tie, while the final gift was a large framed photograph of herself which was passed down the line from the top EMI man at number one in the line-up, to me at the other end. I then went to lean it against the wall when an Embassy official jumped in to tell me that we could not place a picture of Thai royalty on the floor, so I quickly hoisted it up onto the nearest table in order not to cause offence.

But while I had avoided one royal faux-pas in London, I was in for a shock when my boss Bhaskar Menon called me from his office in LA to tell me that he had met with the Princess and she had complained to him about me and something I wrote in our press release about the visit. In it, by way of a compliment, I had compared Princess

Chulabhorn's standing as a recording artist in Thailand to that of Diana Ross and Olivia Newton-John - two world famous multi-million selling artists. Apparently, comparing her to two 'pop singers' was seen as some sort of an insult although Menon, thankfully, didn't take it all that seriously. I have never been to Thailand to find out how they view me over there. Maybe there are photos of me at airports to alert Immigration officials to keep an eye out for me.

For reasons that I can't exactly remember, I was invited to the Football League's centenary dinner in August 1987 despite the fact that the League had been founded in April 1888.

I have no recollection of who invited me and whose table I was on but it was good to find World Champion snooker player Steve Davis sitting alongside me. He is a great fan of music - some of which I liked too but, while I drew the line at French progressive rock band Magma, soul legends like Gene Chandler ('Duke of Earl') were a shared love. The evening at the Grosvenor House Hotel in London ended with the collecting of autographs - for anyone in the music business who loves sport, the real heroes are sports stars - so getting the official centenary programme signed by Davis and the dinner's guest of honour was a double whammy. Did I fail to mention that the main guest was a footballer named Pele who signed with "good luck Pele."

In the aftermath of that dinner, I invited Davis to visit the EMI factory at Hayes to see how records were produced and meet and greet some of the staff. He was in good form, ever charming and smiling, but had to explain to one lady why he didn't smile when he played snooker. A notoriously stony-faced player, he said quite simply, "I bet you don't smile all the time when you're at work, and that was my work and it was serious business."

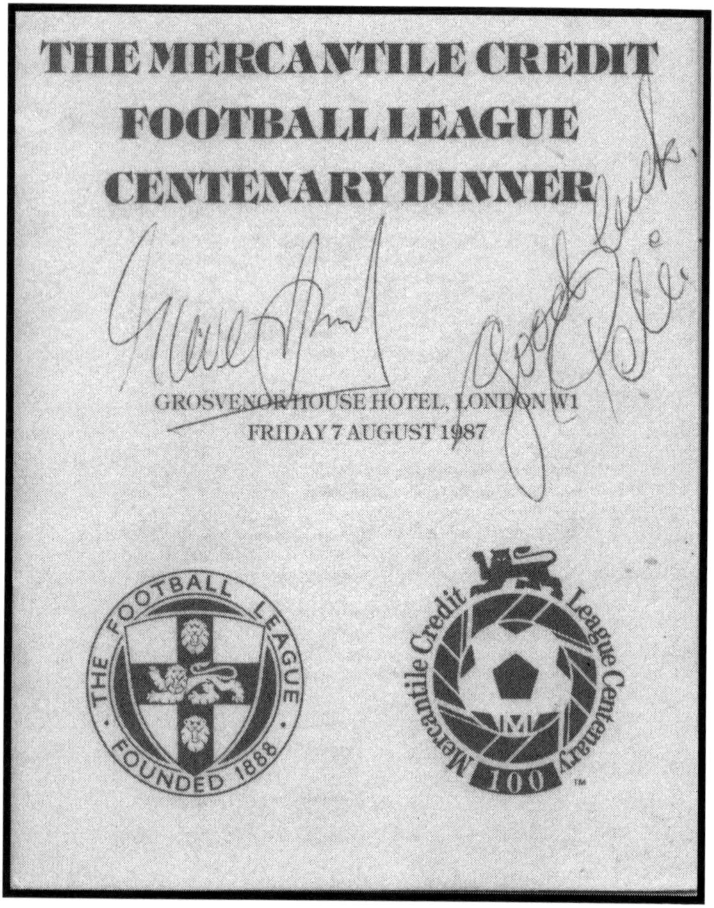

The world's greatest footballer and a world snooker champion celebrated 100 years of football with me

The following year was EMI's 90th birthday, the company having been incorporated in London in 1898, and we celebrated by making a two-part radio programme for BBC Radio 1. It was produced by former BBC and Capital Radio stalwart Tony Hale and I wrote the script and did a load of interviews while Cliff Richard narrated the programmes. When I asked Cliff why he agreed to do it, he said narration was something he had never done before.

The programme featured contributions from Paul McCartney, Tina Turner, Dave Gilmour, the Pet Shops Boys, Kate Bush, Bruce Welch and Mickie Most. I had a walk-on part as the voice of a company spokesman from 1912 reading a note regarding the use of the studio in Hayes when Russian opera singer Feodor Chaliapin was set to record there. It read, spoken by me in the style of Richard Burton with a dash of Noel Coward, "The company bought up all the fowls in the neighbourhood in order to prevent their cackling appearing on the record."

In a nod to both Edgar Allan Poe and George Harrison, we called the programme *The House of Wax*, a phrase Harrison once used to describe EMI. The first hour-long show was broadcast on BBC Radio 1 at 2pm on Saturday November 19 and repeated at 7.30pm the following Tuesday, with the second instalment going out a week later.

There was some media sniping about the BBC broadcasting a programme about EMI written by an executive of the company, which Hale as an independent producer had pitched to the broadcaster.

Gillian Reynolds, the doyen of radio reviewers, wrote in the *Daily Telegraph*, "Eek! It's Cliff Richard telling the story of EMI. Shouldn't the BBC be charging for this kind of promotion?" while the same paper's famous Peterborough diary column suggested that, as the programmes were written by me (an EMI employee) they might "not seem as rigorous in their pursuit of objectivity as might be expected."

The paper also printed a response from BBC Radio 1

about the choice of me as the writer of what was intended as a celebration of the UK's oldest record company rather than an in-depth analysis - that came later in my book *The Rise & Fall of EMI.*

TUESDAY RADIO 22 November

70

1
FM 98-99
London 104-8
MW 1053 + 1089 kHz
285 + 275m

FM stereo all day in London (on 104.8), the North (on 98.8), the Midlands (on 98.4) and South Wales, Avon, Somerset (on 98.7)
News on the half hour from 6.30am until 8.30pm, then 10.30 and 12.30am

5.30am Adrian John

7.00am Simon Mayo
with the Breakfast Crew

9.30am Simon Bates

12.30pm Newsbeat
with Ian Parkinson

12.45pm Gary Davies

3.00pm Steve Wright
Today's lucky numbers are 16, 42 and 31.

5.30pm Newsbeat
with Ian Parkinson

5.45pm Bruno Brookes
looks at this week's Top 40.

7.30pm The House of Wax
Ninety years ago EMI began life as the Gramophone Company. **Cliff Richard**, an EMI artist for 30 years, traces the history of Britain's first record company.
1: *Caruso to Cliff, Not Forgetting Chaliapin*
Written by BRIAN SOUTHALL
Producer TONY RALE
(Broadcast on Saturday at 2.0pm)
● HEAR THIS! *page 31*

8.30pm John Peel

10.30pm Nicky Campbell
goes Into the Night

12.30-2.00am Richard Skinner

2
FM 88-90-2
MW 693 + 909 kHz
433 + 330m

FM stereo 24 hours a day
News on the hour
Headlines 5.30am, 6.30, 7.30, 8.30
Major Bulletins 7.00am, 8.00, 1.00pm, 5.00 and 12 midnight

Sport
Motor Sport: *Lombard RAC Rally* - Harrogate to Carlisle
News at 6.31am, 7.31, 8.31, 10.02, 11.02, 12.02pm, 1.05, 2.02, 3.02, 4.02, 5.05, 6.02, 8.45 (MW), 9.55 and a full round-up at 11.02pm
Sports Round-Up 8.56*am

4.00am Steve Madden
The Early Show

5.30am Chris Stuart
Don't be alarmed - let Chris wake you up.

7.30am Derek Jameson
Morning! Morning!

9.30am Ken Bruce

11.00am Angela Rippon
talks to the people who make the news
with **Dr Bill Dolman** answering listeners' medical queries

1.05pm David Jacobs

2.05pm Gloria Hunniford
including *The Story behind the Song* with today's guest songwriter

3.30pm Adrian Love
Love is in the air. Well, on the air, with some excellent afternoon music.

5.05pm John Dunn
with *Answers Please*
including at 6.45 on *MW only*
Sport and Classified Results

Radio 1, 7.30pm The House of Wax
EMI, 90 years of sound, with a bark as well as a bite

The sinner and the Radi

7.00pm
Steve Race Presents the Radio Orchestra Show
Gordon Langford conducts the **BBC Radio Orchestra** led by MICHAEL TOMALIN
Vocal guest **Scott Peters** with the **BBC Radio Strings** conducted by **Barry Forgie**
With classic album tracks from some of the star vocalists of popular music.
Producer RAY HARVEY

9.00pm
Seven Deadly Singsongs
A series of seven programmes
Third sin: *Anger*
Russell Davies points out the pains and pleasures of sin helped by FRANK SINATRA, BILLIE HOLLIDAY, JAMES TAYLOR and the EVERLY BROTHERS
Producer BARBARA PAGE
● WODDIS ON: *page 109*
9.55 Sports Desk

10.00pm Jazz Score
'Famous son of Gosport celebrates 80 glorious years'
Chairman **Benny Green**
Veterans **Nat Gonella** and **Max Jones** v
Youngsters **Digby Fairweather** and **Alan Elsdon**
Recorded at Gosport Jazz Club, Hampshire
Research and questions by ROY FELLETT
Producer RICHARD WILLCOX

10.30pm
The Name's the Game
During Roger Kitter's absence on board the *QE2*, **Barry Cryer** takes the Chair for another round of the comedy biography game in which **John Junkin** and **Duggie Brown** and their guests **Jeffrey Holland** and **Hilary O'Neil** attempt to sort out who's who.
Biographies compiled and written by TONY HARE
Devised by ROGER KITTER
Producer RICHARD EDIS

11.05pm Brian Matthew
presents **Round Midnight**

The House of Wax radio programme got a mention in the Radio Times

The BBC told the *Telegraph* that there was nothing untoward about the choice of me as writer, although in all honesty I did come with the package as presented by Hale. The corporation explained, "We shall retain editorial control of the programmes. Mr. Southall was commissioned in his capacity as a distinguished author and historian." So there!!

The man who had become head of Thorn EMI in 1987, eight years after Thorn had purchased EMI, was Sir Colin Southgate, and he was very wary of us 'music men'. "They were very secretive and there was a group of music executives who met secretly," he told me.

Having been promoted to the elevated position of Director of Corporate Communications for EMI Worldwide I sat on the board alongside the chairman Bhaskar Menon, plus the bosses of our operations in Europe, Latin America, Asia and America and the people in charge of manufacturing, human resources (it still sounded like a bowel movement to me), music publishing, finance and legal affairs. It was a long way from writing press releases for Batman or even Ray Jackson.

Bhaskar Menon was a high-ranking Indian and the nephew of the country's Defence Minister Krishna Menon who served in the government of Prime Minister Jawaharlal Nehru. He came to EMI from Oxford University - for many years the company took in the cream of the university's graduates as potential executives - and Menon served in London and India before heading up Capitol Records in America. He appointed me to try and strengthen the image of EMI Music in the light of an unsuccessful bid for the company by Gulf & Western before the takeover by Thorn, a company best known for making light bulbs. I was able to hire staff in Los Angeles to help with the situation in

America where, it has to be said, neither EMI nor Thorn were names that meant very much. Capitol Records and the larger Capitol Industries were the main businesses while EMI-America, launched in 1978, gained some status thanks to the likes of Kim Carnes, our old friend Sheena Easton – now resident in the US – J Geils Band and David Bowie. Even so, our reputation in the industry was slipping due to the lack of truly successful global artists. We had big homegrown acts in the UK while America had their best-selling domestic acts but we lacked the huge global superstars such as Michael Jackson, Madonna, Paul Simon and Bruce Springsteen.

Having a Corporate Communications set-up meant we were in the front line to deal with our counterparts in Thorn EMI and also talk to serious financial and business publications such as the *Financial Times, Wall St Journal, Time* and the *Economist* about EMI Music in addition to music business magazines such as *Music Week* and *Billboard*.

I recall that we had little joy in our dealings with the *Wall St Journal*, which perhaps emphasised the point about EMI's poor image in America, but we set Menon up to do a major interview with the *Financial Times* - we were warned by our masters not to include any figures as they were sensitive issues for a company listed on the London Stock Exchange - and he spent many, I think, happy hours with *Economist* journalist Michael Elliott.

Menon had thrived under the 'old' EMI of Lockwood, LG Wood and even Read and had also managed to keep his initial Thorn overlords at arm's length but the situation changed when Southgate became chairman. He was on our case from day one, coming to planning and development meetings to find out what we were doing and why we weren't signing acts that would sell millions. It was explained to him that if we knew who was going to sell millions in the coming year, we would search them out and sign them and, when he asked why we didn't just go out and sign somebody like Phil Collins, we had to further explain that you couldn't just try to tempt acts away from other labels while they were under contract. He was assured that the only people to benefit from that sort of move would be lawyers when they sued our arses. Still, he wasn't convinced that we knew what we were doing and he certainly viewed Menon with a wary eye as our chairman became less and less accessible to his boss.

On one occasion, when Menon had made some excuse for not attending a board meeting, Southgate went as far as to call me and ask where Menon was. I didn't exactly know where he was but was aware that occasionally he would find a meeting with a superstar such as McCartney or one of Floyd or Queen's manager Jim Beach and use that as a reason not to go to a board meeting, safe in the knowledge that Southgate didn't have their numbers and couldn't check up on him. I could only bluster and say I didn't really know Menon's whereabouts and as Southgate persisted, certain that I knew more than I was saying, I had to tell him that it was unfair of him to put me in such an embarrassing position ... Menon was my boss after all.

In the midst of these wranglings with his boss, Menon considered various options for the future of EMI Music and that included a possible merger with a rival major record company. Apparently, he had conversations with Steve Ross, head of the Warner Communications Group, about some sort of a deal and rumour had it that when Menon and three other EMI Music executives were in New York, they hit on the idea of going into the lobby of the Warner

Building and calling Ross to talk directly. The story went that these best laid plans fell apart when the EMI foursome couldn't muster any change for the phone. Is it true? I don't know but wouldn't be surprised to hear that none of the well-paid EMI directors actually carried any cash.

With the Warner plan in ashes, there was another scheme afoot which I found out about at a dinner following my debut appearance at an EMI Music management meeting. There was talk around the table about "the MBO" - something I had never heard of. Trying not to appear dumb, I racked my brain to try and work out what MBO might stand for - an act called the Manhattan Black Orchestra maybe or even More Beatles Outtakes? Fortunately, one of my colleagues went into a lengthy address about the merits of a management buyout (MBO) of EMI Music from Thorn EMI and I was able to give my support to the plan, although nobody had any real idea who would fund it or how Thorn would react. Either way, the topic was never raised again during my time with the company.

Our masters at Thorn EMI were always unreasonably concerned, or at least I thought so, about the fact that EMI was written out in capital letters. It had been that way since it was formed in 1931 and still appeared in CAPS when it was tagged alongside Thorn after their take-over. I recall attending 'branding' meetings when the Thorn logo was on the agenda and there were concerns about it looking less like a 'thorn' and more an upside down drawing pin while some thought it was all too phallic. And then came the debate about why couldn't the name Thorn be written in capital letters like EMI and it didn't take a genius - it could have been me - to point out that it was somebody's name (Sir Jules Thorn who founded the company) and not an acronym.

There was a certain amount of jealousy within the ranks of Thorn's senior management that EMI didn't just have a BIGGER name but also a better history and that resulted in the petty theft of the original HMV (His Master's Voice) painting by Francis Barraud from 1899 of the dog (Nipper) and trumpet, although it was originally painted with a phonograph cylinder machine not a gramophone. It was removed from the London offices of EMI Music and displayed in Thorn EMI's headquarters alongside some other historic artefacts from the EMI archive. Not quite on the same scale, but there were echoes of the case of the Elgin marbles.

Maybe Colin Southgate did get wind of the MBO plot, as very soon after he set about reforming EMI Music by hiring a former General Mills and CBS/Fox executive to be president and chief operating officer of EMI Music Worldwide and successor to Menon who I'm not sure was kept in the loop about the appointment.

New man Jim Fifield wasn't overly keen on any of us who were close to Menon and, in addition to buying the music publishing business SBK Entertainment for a reported $295 million, Chrysalis Records for £79 million and Virgin Music for £560 million, a number of 'bag men' were shown the door in one way or another.

However, before the clear-out, a handful of EMI Music execs, including me, got together to try to hatch a revolution and get rid of Fifield by telling Southgate we refused to work for the new man in town. Of course, it came to nothing but ironically two of the ringleaders stayed on to further their careers in a big way. However, the 'uprising' ended before it began and some of us were eventually left out in the cold.

I was not on Fifield's 'to keep' list so, in 1989 after 15 years almost to the day, I left and was given a gold HMV Dog &

Trumpet lapel badge, which I should have been given after 10 years' service but - hey - better late than never. I was also called up by somebody in accounts telling me that I had expenses running into hundreds of pounds against advances which I had to pay back to the company. I disputed this on the basis that the one thing I was meticulous about was my expenses which, while they may have contained a few 'dodgy' claims, always matched and usually exceeded any advances I had taken out. My final words on the matter were to tell the 'money man' to sue me as I was out of the door on Friday. I never heard another word.

My time with Bhaskar Menon was littered with fond memories. Knowing that I didn't get on with Indian food, he was always keen to take me to his favourite haunts in London and LA where, he assured me, he would order the mildest of mild curries for me ... and sometimes he did. However, I knew my place when lunching with him and singer José Feliciano as they sort of went off-menu and began sharing a brown paper bag of raw potent chillies. Maybe they were a side order in the deal that brought the Puerto Rican to EMI.

Menon was still there when I left and as a going away present he hosted a slap-up dinner in London, gave me a desktop computer (plus my office chair which suited my dodgy back) and a trip to the States to say farewell to my staff and colleagues in LA. And, to top it off, he signed off on a flight from New York to London on Concorde during which I collected as many souvenirs as I could. If it wasn't stuck down I pocketed it.

Then came a surprise leaving gift from the man who asked for me to be fired way back in 1983 - Paul McCartney. He had either forgotten or forgiven me, as he sent over signed copies of my *Abbey Road* book, with his foreword, and the book *The Complete Beatles Recording Sessions* which I had edited, and they came with surprisingly warm dedications. In *Abbey Road* he wrote: "Thanks Brian, for all your help. All the best" and then signed it and added a smiley face drawing. In *The Complete Beatles* book he put: "To Brian, TA! With fab best wishes and good luck" This time there was just a signature and no drawing but I was happy with that.

A fond farewell from a grateful Paul McCartney when I left EMI

Chapter 16

THE BRITS AND OTHER AWARDS

The annual BRIT Awards are now a fixture in the music calendar but they actually began with a one-off show back in 1977 which was a double celebration of Thomas Edison's invention of the phonograph and recorded sound in 1877, and Queen Elizabeth II's Silver Jubilee.

It's extraordinary, looking back, to think that I was there that night in October at the Wembley Conference Centre when awards were handed out for the best records and artists over the 25 year period from 1952. Unsurprisingly, The Beatles took home three prizes (Best Group, Best Album *(Sgt Pepper)* and for Outstanding Contribution) while Cliff Richard was Best Male and Shirley Bassey Top Female. Best Single was shared between Queen ('Bohemian Rhapsody') and Procol Harum ('A Whiter Shade Of Pale') and, while both groups turned up, only Procol Harum performed alongside Cliff Richard, George Martin and the Wembley Conference Orchestra and amazingly Americans Simon & Garfunkel, who also won prizes for both Best International Album and Single with *Bridge Over Troubled Water.*

Broadcast on Thames TV, the show attracted 11.2 million viewers which, in the near 30 years up until 2004 when I was involved with the show, remained the top viewing figure, closely followed by 11.1 million in 1996.

Perhaps as a sign of the times, the warm-up on that night back in 1977 was comedian and scriptwriter Barry Cryer while the guests of honour were Tony Blackburn, Nicholas Parsons and Frankie Howerd – don't ask me why. It was also the event that saw the introduction of Britannia in the official title of the show - The British Record Industry Britannia Centenary Awards. In fact the name Britannia could be only used with the express permission of the Bank Of England who generously sent along a penny from 1700 which was incorporated into the award design.

After a five year gap, the British Record Industry Awards returned and while the official history of the show, which I wrote in 2004, notes that the 1977 event was the first, there were those closely involved with the 1982 show who reckoned that this was when it all began. However, the annual prize giving actually became the BRIT Awards in 1990 - in honour of Britannia whose image had featured on the awards since 1987.

Beginning in 1990, I took on the role of editor of the official BRIT Awards magazine - a position I held for a decade or more - and it was my job to interview past winners, hosts and nominees to go along with the lists of official nominations. And I have to say it was fun as almost all the acts I approached were willing and able to talk. Maybe they thought that if they didn't take part, they might get a black mark against their name when it came to the final vote.

Back in 1990 Jonathan King was producing his debut BRITs show and for reasons best known to himself, he decided to include Prime Minister Margaret Thatcher. She was to be filmed in 10 Downing Street as one of a number of well-known figures talking about their favourite record. At least that was how King sold the idea to John Whittingdale MP who was Mrs Thatcher's Private Secretary at the time, who later told me: "He sold it to me and I advised the Prime Minister that it would be a good thing for her to do in terms of profile. So then we decided that her favourite record would be 'Memory' by Andrew Lloyd Webber and sung by Elaine Paige - I knew she knew it and liked the show and it was a good English song." The MP for Maldon in Essex added, "King suddenly asked about music from her younger days and I suddenly thought that wasn't in the script, we haven't thought about this. She came up with Ivor Novello and 'We'll Gather Lilacs' and then he asked about songs from when the children were young and she said 'Telstar' - (pause) - by The Beatles - such a marvellous tune'. Now it was beginning to go horribly wrong and finally she said there was a song Mark and Carol listened to when they were about six and that's when we got to 'How Much Is That Doggie In the Window?'"

When it came to show time, Whittingdale was in for an even bigger shock. "Of course the video wasn't what King had pledged at all. There was nobody else in the film, all the other so-called public figures had disappeared and when they just showed Margaret Thatcher talking about these songs with some ridiculous black and white footage to go with it; the whole audience was in hysterics."

King did save some of the PM's blushes by editing out the words The Beatles and showing a film of the Tornados performing their hit 'Telstar', and Whittingdale survived to tell the tale and become, not just a Tory MP but also, Secretary of State for Culture, Media & Sport. He finished by telling me, "I remember thinking 'Oh God this is a complete disaster'. The only good thing was that she didn't watch the show so she never knew about it." And he added that he was confident that nobody would ever have the nerve to mention it to the Prime Minister.

In one of many BRIT 'moments', Thatcher's appearance brought a sharp response from double award winners Fine Young Cannibals who returned their trophies to the organisers explaining, "It's wrong and inappropriate for us to be associated with what amounts to a photo-opportunity for Margaret Thatcher and the Conservative party."

In 1991 the production of the brochure involved me typing out the text for the magazine and handing it over to the design company to re-set for the final version. The young man given that task was of a certain age and not a music buff and managed to insert the names RON Orbison and STRING into the copy. Fortunately, both mistakes were spotted before printing but we all wondered whether Roy Orbison and Sting would ever have made it with their alternative 'new' identities.

One of my great heroes, Van Morrison was presented with the award for Outstanding Contribution to British Music (quite rightly) in 1994 but it's not a night I recall with great joy as I got oh so close to chatting with Van the Man. My wife and I were in conversation with his manager - with Van seated at a table just behind him - when he asked if we had ever met Van. I said "no never" and his manager came back with the line, "That's a pity because he's not meeting people tonight." If I had been quicker I would have quipped (annoyingly) "That's a coincidence because, neither am I."

1996 was the year when Michael Jackson appeared in the show and had his performance interrupted by Pulp's Jarvis Cocker who protested by jumping on the stage and waggled his bum. It was a curious protest that wasn't actually broadcast as the cameras were focussed on Jackson singing, but it did get Cocker arrested but eventually released without charge. After the show, Jackson sat in an editing suite looking at the footage of his performance, but before he talked about his concerns with BRIT executives he unscrewed the heads from all the microphones in the suite so nobody could tape or hear the conversation. Apparently, he was worried about his make-up in some of the shots and a lot of time and money was then spent hiring the latest video technology to put it right in the middle of the night. However, somebody who was there told me that the singer's real concern was the fact that in some shots you could actually see Jackson's facial skeleton as a result of his plastic surgery.

Three years on I popped down to a rehearsal studio in South London to interview Robbie Williams who was up for three awards - Best Male, Best Album and Best Singles. He found me an hour in his schedule for a chat for the magazine and in addition to telling me how he wouldn't rest "until I've dominated the world," he agreed to respond to five descriptions of himself ... and this is what we got.

Cheeky chappie ... "well I am aren't I"

Showman ... "yeah, definitely"

Party animal ... "errr – yeah"

Heart throb ... "I don't wake up in the morning and go 'morning heart throb'"

Hard & soft rocker ... "I'm a hard rocker with a soft centre, just like a coffee cream."

Before we finished, I asked him to sign a good luck card for my daughter as she was taking her management accountancy exams the next day. He obliged and she took it with her - and failed! But she qualified with flying colours a few months later and has gone on from there to forge a successful career in money with or without Robbie's blessing.

The following year I interviewed ex-Spice Girl Geri Halliwell for the BRIT Awards magazine and from the very beginning it was an odd telephone chat. As we started she insisted on knowing my birthday and my star sign and, presumably deciding our stars were in some way compatible, we continued. I did a quick check and while I am a Cancer and apparently "intuitive and can exist in both emotional and material realms" (who knew?), Halliwell is a Leo which seemingly makes her "passionate, loyal and dramatic." In all my years as a writer she is the only person ever to want to know this.

Having huge numbers of famous musicians in one place at each and every BRIT Awards show was always going to bring out the worst in some but all the tales from backstage in 1999 were about an American singer. It seemed that Whitney Houston's 'diva-ish' behaviour stunned everybody as a phalanx of menacing bodyguards accompanied her from the backstage area to the stage. Anyone silly enough to get in her way was swept aside unceremoniously.

The backstage area often featured small individual chalets or bungalows or sheds and one year two of the world's biggest stars had a competition to see who could get the best and biggest floral arrangement for their temporary garden while Prince, already noted for his notoriously quirky behaviour, insisted on a an all-white dressing room - everything in there from crockery, sofas, chairs, tables, cushions, throws, tissues (and boxes) - had to be pure white, while he dressed in all white - presumably to blend in ... or hide.

Looking at a list of the shows' hosts over the years is an

interesting exercise to note who was 'big' and when. In my time - between 1977 and 2004 - we had Michael Aspel, David Jacobs, Tim Rice, Noel Edmonds, Jonathan King, Sam Fox & Mick Fleetwood, Cathy McGowan, Simon Bates (voice-over) Richard O'Brien, Elton John & Ru Paul, Chris Evans, Ben Elton, Johnny Vaughan, Davina McCall, Ant & Dec, Zoe Ball & Frank Skinner and Cat Deeley. Hands up if you are too young to know who some of these people are – or were.

My official history of the BRIT awards was never made available for sale in bookshops which was a shame. Copies were available at the show or ordered from the BPI (British Phonographic Industry) but delays in deciding whether to produce it or not and when to publish it (not my decisions) made it a hard commercial proposition… or so I was told.

Some years later, I decided it was time for me to remove my name from the voting panel for the BRIT Awards which included industry folk, journalists, DJs and other 'influencers'. I knew it was time when looking at that year's list of British Male and Female Artists I could only recognise Ian Brown and Van Morrison. And they weren't going to win - so I hung up my ballot paper.

Never intended as competition to the BRIT Awards, a collection of record company bosses and executives from the IFPI (International Federation of Phonographic Industries) decided that sales in Europe should be recognized in some way. The answer was the IFPI Platinum Awards when prizes were given to artists who sold a million copies of any album throughout Europe. Introduced in 1996, the award ceremonies were held in Brussels every two years as part of a larger campaign concerning European Copyright Legislation, which the record industry was trying to get amended, and over the years the great and good of the global music industry assembled in the capital of Belgium. Acts such as Luciano Pavarotti, Blue, Emma Bunton, Texas, Robbie Williams, INXS, Italy's Laura Pausini, Westernhagen from Germany, Axelle Red from Belgium and the Scandinavian duo Aqua turned up to collect and, in some cases perform, but there was one multi-million selling American group who weren't so keen.

During their 1995 European tour, R.E.M were invited by Warner Music International's (WMI) marketing people to receive their prize for selling over a million copies of the album *Monster.* As a consultant to WMI, I was the company's representative on the IFPI awards committee and it fell to me to get the invitation to the band for them to travel to Belgium to pick up their prize. However, I was informed that they weren't in any mood to accept an award anywhere - in Brussels or London - for an album they, apparently, didn't think was one of their best and they didn't really want to be seen celebrating it. While it would have been a major coup to get the band (or any one of them) to attend and a prize giving photo with Messrs Berry, Buck, Mills and Stipe would have been nice, everyone at the record company was just thankful that music fans in eight countries - from Sweden to New Zealand (including the UK and the US) - disagreed about the album, took it to number one in their charts and justified the expensive marketing campaign.

The lobbying of Euro MPs was also on the agenda so the most senior members of the European Parliament were among the guests at the show and those of us on the committee were required to come up with artists to attend and even perform. Alongside the awards, the efforts to make the copyright case to politicians involved us pulling in artists like Jean-Michel Jarre and the Corrs to act as industry spokespeople. I took Andrea, Sharon, Caroline and Jim Corr to Strasbourg to perform in the Parliament buildings canteen for a bunch of Euro MPs including Irish Euro MP and former singer Dana. My abiding memory is of a lackey coming up to her during our conversation and giving her a message. The Eurovision Song Contest winner (circa 1970) then turned to me and said, "You'll have to excuse me, the Bishop of Dublin is on the phone." Dana wasn't the only celebrity-turned-politician who we involved. Greek singer Nana Mouskouri was a supporter, as was Italian film legend Gina Lollobrigida, who was keen to change copyright laws in the film industry.

My two main contributions to all this were getting the Corrs on board, although now's the time to admit that I only ever referred to Jim by name as I could never work out which of the girls was which, and inviting Phil Collins to act as the show's host in 2000 alongside Neil Kinnock, Vice President of the European Commission.

The Music Industry Trust Awards (MIT) have taken place since 1992 and recognize people who have made an outstanding contribution to the British Music Industry. The awards night is a glamorous affair, where music industry executives and artists gather together to eat, drink and honour an individual. Among the winners over the years have been Sir George Martin, Elton John & Bernie Taupin (seen as one), Kylie Minogue, Harvey Goldsmith and Simon Cowell but the night in 2000 when Ahmet Ertegun, the founder of Atlantic Records, was the winner holds a place in my memory.

This particular evening took its place among the finest memorable moments during the time I worked with a host of stars and superstars. Among the unforgettable encounters I'd count a few of them as spending time with two of the Beatles, meeting Bob Dylan in a London street with his press officer and having a conversation during which he said nothing at all, 'going out' with Kate Bush and being involved in the Sex Pistols fiasco.

Then, at the glitzy MIT event, I found myself sitting at an Atlantic Records table where I was placed between Phil Collins and Eric Clapton. I knew Phil but not Eric and after we had a more than pleasant chat, it became apparent that they needed to talk to each other rather than across me – so we swapped seats in a polite and organised fashion. On the table behind us sat Sir Michael Caine, one of my acting heroes - think *Alfie, Zulu, The Man Who Would Be King, Educating Rita, The Quiet Man* - with his wife and I was moved, as we stood next to each other, to tell him how much I admired his work. I didn't embarrass him or me by asking for an autograph - I should have - but after nodding and saying thank you, he shared these words with me, "Sorry but I gotta go and have a piss." And he delivered the line beautifully.

Chapter 17

CONSULTANT 'BY APPOINTMENT' WELL ALMOST

Despite being cut from EMI after 15 years, I still believed that I had a future in the music business. You could argue that it was all I knew but either way I decided to set up a PR consultancy business and my first two clients were a former EMI boss and a friend from my teenage years as a cub reporter.

I chose to name my company BS Ink (as in bullshit and ink) and had business cards printed and a small name plate made for my front door - it was some sort of legal requirement. I found that the email address I used back then, 'bsink', created confusion when I gave it out over the phone to people or businesses. They thought I was a plumber!

Having been responsible for corporate PR for EMI Music, I had no desire to go anywhere near rock stars and do 'press' for them as they expected the world to sit up and pay attention not just to promote their records and shows but also listen to their thoughts on a range of unrelated subjects. I knew that being a star's press officer was just a few steps down from being their manager and we all knew what that meant - calls in the middle of the night from hotels asking how you called room service or stopped maids stealing underwear from the laundry as souvenirs. I could name names but I won't.

I was a 'company' man in the broadest sense and my former boss at EMI Records, Ramon Lopez was the first to come a-calling. He offered me a role as a consultant to Warner Music International (WMI) which was based in London and was responsible for the activities of the mighty Warner Music empire outside the USA.

Warner Music included the legendary Warner Bros., Atlantic, Elektra and Asylum record companies and was part of Warner Communications until it merged in 1989 with Time Inc. to form Time Warner and become the largest media company in the world. I was joining as a two day a week consultant to Lopez and his team based in Baker Street - where I had an office - and working with the existing Communications executive Tracy Nicholas Bledsoe who was based in New York where WMI also had offices.

At around the same time my old friend from Chelmsford, Stuart McAllister, decided he needed me to help him develop the image of HMV's retail operations which he was keen to expand into an international business. This was a one day a week role which I did from my home office with occasional trips to HMV's headquarters in Henley-on-Thames.

McAllister and I knew each other from my time on the local *Essex Chronicle* newspaper when, in the weekly pop column, I reviewed gigs by his band Lee Scott and The Roulettes in addition to playing football against him. After not seeing each other for nearly 40 years, he pitched up at a

Thorn EMI executive gathering as the chairman of the HMV Group, while I was still at EMI Music. I was able to smooth the way for him to work with EMI's music companies and he repaid the debt by retaining me as a consultant.

Now I had two clients paying me more for working three days a week than my final salary at EMI Music but, on the downside, there was no company car, private medical cover or pensions. On the upside, along with the expenses, I got to travel to New York and Los Angeles to meet with people at the Warner Music companies which brought me into contact with some of the biggest names in the music business - Warner Bros. Records boss Mo Ostin, Ahmet and Nehusi Ertegun, the founders of Atlantic, Seymour Stein who ran Sire and Jac Holzman who launched Elektra. In fact it was Holzman who, in his role as the company's chief technologist, I met first when he introduced me to whatever was new or about to be new in the world of music delivery post-CDs. I can't remember what it was I was looking at but Holzman was a bigger fan of technology than me.

By the time we had moved into the nineties, I was doing three days a week at Warner Music International and had been granted a bigger and better office - in fact I was now on the top floor alongside Lopez where his office was only marginally bigger than mine. We shared the floor with his personal assistant Sandra Manning - who had been with him at EMI - an occasional second secretary (who also helped me out on now and again) plus a kitchen with a chef and butler and, of course, an executive dining room. It was too glamorous for words and I revelled in my new-found luxury in a giant office which, oddly, was directly across the road from the old Baker Street offices where I worked for Tamla Motown two decades earlier. Then it was three people to an office the size of a BIG cupboard.

It was Mrs. Manning who persuaded me to try out Virgin Atlantic for a trip we were both making to New York. It was my debut in Upper Class and it has to be said that I immediately became a fan of Mr. Branson's airline. That was until the plane started to break down over Ireland and we had to return to Gatwick for plan B. This involved a return walk through customs - "We haven't been anywhere to buy anything illegal or otherwise" - was the cry that went up as we trooped back into the departure lounge. It transpired that Gatwick is what is called a 'silent' airport and has no tannoy or public address system so, after a long wait, a man from Virgin stood on a table and eventually told us Upper Class passengers that we could board the next flight to New York which would go via Boston but, he warned, "Don't leave the plane with the other passengers at Boston or you'll never get back on board." I have no idea what happened to the non-Upper Class passengers but we finally arrived in New York on just about the same day as we left the UK.

It wasn't a great Virgin debut and Mrs. Manning wrote to Branson to point out that his Virgin ground staff were very thin on the ground staff and it was all a bit frustrating. She also mentioned my name in the dispatch - I had met Branson when he was still heading up Virgin Records - and that it was my first flight with his airline.

I had put the whole thing behind me until the phone rang at home and a man identifying himself as Richard Branson apologised for the delays and lack of information and added a few thousand air miles to my account. It struck me that I never got a call from Lord King when any of my British Airways flights were held up.

Now, with only two clients, I was also free to get involved with other industry organisations such as the British Radio

Academy which began in 1983 to recognize and support UK broadcasting. I sat on the board alongside the head of BBC Radio 1, Johnny Beerling, the former head of Capital Radio, Tim Blackmore, and my former BBC and Capital radio producer friend Tony Hale, amongst others, as we tried to make radio, particularly music radio, more attractive.

The trips to New York (and I was now a dedicated Virgin man) to liaise with the communications people in both WMI, Warner Music and even Time Warner became more frequent as Ramon Lopez set about expanding WMI by opening new operations and adding local companies. In its first 20 years, from its founding in 1970, WMI boasted a total of 28 labels and joint ventures around the world. In the five years from 1990 a total of 17 companies and new labels were added to gain further international coverage … and every one of them required a press release.

I spent a long time concocting words and phrases to explain the WMI philosophy along with announcements about the executives who came and went in this period of expansion. And when it became time to celebrate the company's 25th anniversary in 1995, I was given the task of creating a brochure for global distribution telling the story of WMI. It was glossy, well-illustrated and included messages from the most senior executives at Time Warner and the Warner Music Group but I bet they never spotted the not-so-deliberate mistake.

The production of the magazine coincided with me travelling the world to create another brochure as part of HMV's 75th anniversary celebration. This involved visiting operations in Europe, Asia, Australia, Canada and America and while I was away on this jaunt (sorry, fact-finding mission) the final proofs of the WMI publication came up for approval. I think they reached me during a stopover in Vancouver on my way to Toronto and I sort of 'signed off' on them, but left it to people in New York and then the designers in London to do the final checking.

That was where it all went wrong as, between us, we missed one glaring error which wasn't just a spelling mistake or a badly-worded caption but the wrong flag to go with the country's alphabetical entry. Korea appeared after Japan and before Malaysia but - and it couldn't have been more politically incorrect - with the flag of North Korea. I was quite rightly blamed and (not so rightly) mocked for the error by some senior staff and I offered my resignation to Lopez but he not only refused it but took it on himself to ensure the 'mockers' and 'knockers' ceased the mocking and knocking. For reasons I still do not understand, the company based in Seoul was opened as Warner Music Korea and not WM South Korea which would probably have alerted the design team who put the brochure together to use the right flag but as they were all far too young to have been taught about the 'demilitarised zone' or the '38th parallel', which ran in part along the border between South and North Korea, it was not to be. The man most pissed off about it all was the head of WM Korea who had to stick the right flag over the offending entry in order to use the brochures he had been sent.

Music industry trade shows under the banner Midem (Marche International du Disque l'Edition Musicale) had been operating since 1967 (when it was advertised as the first Record & Music Publishing Market) and usually took place in France but in 1995 the first get-together to take place in Asia was held in Hong Kong. One of the highlights was see how those in the know about Feng Shui attempted to make sure that something like 50 or more music company booths created the right balance with the natural world.

I was there with the WMI delegation and on the agenda was an appearance by Chinese artist Dadawa whose debut album caused something of a stir in the UK. She was born in Guangzhou in China, and her album *Sister Drum*, which WMI released internationally, featured music from Tibet and pictured her dressed in traditional Tibetan robes. This caused some concern in China but brought protests nearer home from the London-based Free Tibet group opposed to China's occupation of the country and the Dalai Lama's forced exile in India. I met her in Hong Kong and a couple of us had a translated conversation with her about the situation, but she was adamant she had sympathy for the people of Tibet and her album was a way of showing her support. Despite the protests, her album was the first Asian compact disc to sell over a million copies in China.

Meanwhile, the album became something of an issue closer to home as the cover photograph offended a whole bunch of people in the UK and they bombarded the WMI offices in Baker Street with letters protesting about Dadawa, her album and criticising us for releasing it. Among those we offended were University lecturers, who wrote on college headed notepaper, and others who had sympathy for the Tibetan cause.

We took the view, as we always did with any controversial albums or lyrics, that unless things broke the laws of obscenity, slander (spoken or sung) or libel (written), we did not act as censors. My role in all this was to draft a letter outlining our views about freedom of speech and an individual's right to air their opinion in words or actions within the law.

Now that the protesters had a name to focus on, the letters came addressed to me personally and while there were no threats of violence there was a warning that there would be a protest outside our Baker Street offices late in the afternoon on a particular day. We had no idea how many were going to turn up so on the advice of our legal team, we informed the local constabulary in case they were needed to keep the streets clear or, more importantly, accompany me to the tube station. In the end, the protest sort of fizzled out as something of a damp squib on a very wet afternoon.

When I left the office that day there was a constable sitting in reception waiting for me but he didn't seem overly concerned for my safety as there was just one lone protester outside the office holding a placard in one hand and an umbrella in the other. Thinking that it was highly unlikely that he knew what I looked like, I dismissed my police escort and walked off into the night.

Midem 2001 was held in Cannes, the luxury seaside resort in the South of France, when the recipient of their Person of the Year award was award-winning songwriter and producer David Foster. As his 143 Records label was licensed through the Warner Music Group and through his work with Atlantic signings The Corrs, a team of us WMI people took a table at the formal dinner.

It was a star-studded occasion where Josh Groban sang for his supper while the rest of us wined and dined ... some to excess. With Foster that night was a lawyer from his 143 company who was also the brother of his then wife who in turn was a former girl-friend of Elvis Presley. Linda Thompson left Presley in 1976, after four years together, and a year before his death. During that time, her brother Sam Thompson, a local sheriff's officer, became part of Presley's entourage as a bodyguard and stayed on after his sister's break-up. Having studied law and eventually qualified as a judge, Thompson moved to Los Angeles to join Foster's company and over a drink in a fancy Riviera bar, he told me his story of the days at Graceland following Presley's death in August 1977. Amid rumours of people planning to steal Presley's body and other more bizarre ones that he was not dead but had chosen to disappear to live a quiet life away from the rock'n'roll hullabaloo, his bodyguards kept watch over The King while he lay in a coffin in Graceland.

Thompson was one of the select band of people given the task of watching over Presley's body during the night and as he sat in a room in the Presley family home, he thought about the stories about Presley's non-death. "I was sitting there with a hurricane lamp and shotgun on my lap and I looked over at Elvis lying in his coffin and said, 'If you ain't dead, now's the time to tell me boy'."

My time as a consultant with Warner Music International - and eventually my appointment as permanent Vice President of Communications - ran from 1989 to 2003 and included a visit to the Rock and Roll Hall of Fame 9th annual induction dinner held in 1994 in New York's Waldorf Astoria Hotel, where I had had dinner with Queen two decades earlier.

Among the Inductees that year were The Band, Grateful Dead, Chuck Berry, Willie Dixon, Duane Eddy, Elton John plus John Lennon and the Animals. Lennon's honour was collected by Yoko Ono and Paul McCartney in what looked like a slightly difficult coming together moment, while the Animals were there in numbers but minus singer Eric Burdon who reportedly sent a note explaining that he had a paying gig that night in Germany.

That night the star-packed audience at the art deco hotel, which opened in 1931, witnessed a number of one-off performances as guest artists got together to perform, among others, two Lennon & McCartney songs. The Band and Eric Clapton offered up 'The Weight' while Axl Rose and Bruce Springsteen got together to sing 'Come Together' but the finale was a tribute to Willie Dixon with the Grateful Dead, Chuck Berry, Bruce Hornsby and Dixon's daughter Shirley banging out 'Wang Dang Doodle'. Nights like that don't come along too often so it was one for the memory bank.

In the run-up to the 1994 World Cup football tournament in the USA, WMI signed a deal to release the second *Three Tenors* album which was to be recorded live in Los Angeles on the eve of the football championships. Somewhere along the line I was asked about a good PR company WMI could hire to promote the recording featuring, once again, Luciano Pavarotti, Placido Domingo and Jose Carreras. I opted for Laister Dixon which was being run by PR experts Wendy Laister and Bernard Doherty and, when the work was done on the Tenors, we hatched a plan to form a new company with me joining them.

The deal was that we each brought in a set amount of accounts or billing to make it work but when I approached Ramon Lopez about the idea, he was reluctant to let his communications needs be handled by an outside operation -- even if I was involved. That put an abrupt end to the plan but not before we had come up with a name for the new outfit ... Laister, Southall, Doherty could become LSD with its various connotations!

The WMI conferences knocked the EMI efforts into a cocked hat as we travelled to Madrid, Boston, Montreux, Hong Kong, Sydney and Barcelona for week-long events involving presentations (many of which I wrote), dinners and shows – oh, and great presents including high grade Cartier watches, luxury leather cases from Loewe, hand-blown Swiss glassware and some wonderfully unique Aboriginal paintings. This artwork was obviously handed out in Sydney but it was sad to see that some of the highest ranking (and wealthiest) executives from our sister American companies could not be bothered to get them securely wrapped and sent back in the hold as checked baggage.

So what did they do? They just left paintings worth anything up to $500 in their rooms (or suites) for us to collect and take back to London without ever telling chairman Ramon Lopez who would have been both upset and insulted.

My painting by Susi Petyarre, whose work has been exhibited in the UK, Germany and SE Asia and displayed in Australian art galleries, hangs in a prominent place in my home.

The WMI event in Barcelona in 2002 was my last conference appearance as a senior executive with the company but it was not without merit. When I arrived in the hotel - albeit a day late as I was at my good friend radio producer Tony Hale's wedding on the opening day - I was greeted by the chairman of the Warner Music Group, Roger Ames, who was sitting in the lobby chatting with somebody I didn't recognize.

Ames had been a colleague of mine back at EMI Records nearly 30 years earlier but now he was my (and thousands of others) big boss. He called me over and introduced me to Malcolm Gladwell who he said was an author and then he told Gladwell that I too was an author. It was obvious to me that he had no idea who I was or what books I had written but I was in the same position – I had no idea who he was or what he had published.

It turned out that he was a guest speaker at the conference on the back of his best-selling 2000 book *Tipping Point*, which seemingly focused on the "mysterious sociological changes that mark everyday life." Our brief meeting was a pleasant enough encounter but when I got to my room, I discovered a copy of the book among my welcome pack. Everybody had one and we were all supposed to read it. Even though I didn't know if there would be questions or an essay writing competition later, I never actually delved into it and when I left WMI, I think I probably left it for whoever took over my office. Sorry Malcolm but I bet you've still never read any of my efforts.

Before I invited Phil Collins to host the IFPI Platinum Awards show in Brussels, I spent time with him at the Fisher Lane Farm studios owned by Genesis in Chiddingfold, Surrey, where he spoke to me for a WMI in-house magazine feature. And, apart from talking about music and his various solo releases for WMI, he threw into the conversation his shopping exploits in the local Sainsbury's supermarket. It seemed that he and his then wife were regular visitors to the store for their weekly shop despite his day job as a rock'n'roll star. "The first time it was difficult as people kept asking me for my autograph", he explained before adding, "But by about the third time we went, they were all bored with me and just said to anyone who asked 'oh, he's in here all the time'." Years earlier I had had a similar conversation with Cliff Richard and he said almost exactly the same with the only difference being that he was a Waitrose man.

My next Phil Collins moment came in the summer of 1998 when I went to see him and his Big Band play at the Royal Festival Hall where they performed hits by both Genesis and Collins alongside some jazz standards. It has to be said that it wasn't the best show I'd ever been to – hearing 'Sussudio' and 'Invisible Touch' given a big band treatment just didn't work for me ... and I wasn't the only one left disappointed.

Me and Phil Collins discuss supermarket shopping

During the interval, my producer friend Tony Hale and I went to the gents where we stood next to Sir George Martin (it would be the last time I saw him) and I enquired, "Enjoying the gig, George?" He turned his head and said, "Tremendous fun chaps. Mind you I'm as deaf as a post so that probably helps."

For the next instalment of the Brian and Phil story, the great man wasn't even there and to this day does not know how much help I was to him in his career. When his solo collection *Hits* album came out, I was asked to stand in and provide a guide voice-over for a TV advert WMI were creating to send out to their various companies around the world. I had a script which I delivered perfectly (to my mind) alongside the visuals and this was then sent to the local companies who would get their own person to provide the commentary in their local language. I left the studio happy with my evening's work.

A year later, the head of Warner Music Canada thanked

me for the voice over which they said worked perfectly for them. They had not bothered to hire anyone to add a commentary but went with my guide vocal on a nationwide TV campaign. I assumed they were so impressed with my work that they decided it couldn't be bettered by a Canadian voice artist until the company chief explained, "No, it was cheaper to use you as you were free." However, I still take some credit for the album going four times platinum in Canada but I've got a feeling the cheque is still in the post.

Continuing in my life as a consultant, there was an unexpected day out when I was in LA to spend professional time with my communications counterpart at the Warner Music Group and relax by hanging out at a fancy hotel near Rodeo Drive, one of the world's most expensive streets. I can't recall the name of the hotel but I do remember sunning myself by the pool when a young boy came up to me and asked, "May I spray you sir?" Somewhat perplexed and taken aback by the offer, I asked "With what, where and why?" He then produced an aerosol spray full of cold water which he proceeded to flit across my front and back. The next day he was back but this time he was offering me frozen grapes. There is another world out there.

Apart from time by the pool, there was the unexpected offer of a trip to the Warner Bros. studio lot (on Warner Boulevard no less) for the meeting of great PR minds, which provided two other memorable moments. I was invited into the inner sanctum of Bob Daly, the chairman of both Warner Bros. and the Warner Music Group, which required me to pass by three secretaries in two separate offices.

Daly held court in the cavernous office previously used by the legendary film executive Jack Warner and I was told it came complete with secret passages that led to the dressing rooms of aspiring young actresses. But, on the day

I was there, Daly was more interested in my view of a senior WMI executive who was about to be "let go." He wondered what I thought of the person and how his departure might affect company morale. When I had said my bit, Daly said he had done his homework, talked to some executives and managers and come to the conclusion that some people thought the man was a genius while others thought he was a "bit of a shit." That was when Daly, who was married to singer/songwriter Carole Bayer Sager and might have got some inside music biz gen, said that he sided with the latter and within weeks the WMI man was gone.

Before I left the Warner Bros. lot as I was given the five dollar tour (for nothing) and we walked through the artificial streets that I had seen in hundreds of movies until we finally arrived at a small basketball court with just one hoop on a wall. That was when I was told it was where George Clooney played when he was filming *ER* back in the nineties. And there wasn't even a plaque.

During my time with WMI, I was also retained by two UK based trade organisations – the British Phonographic Industry (BPI) and the International Federation of the Phonographic Industry (IFPI) - although they were only brief excursions as a temporary stand-in between full time appointments. I can't remember what the pressing issues were within the BPI when I came off the sub's bench to help out, although changing the copyright laws for recorded music was always an issue and was eventually upped from 50 years to 70 years in 2013. The same issue was at near the top of the IFPI's agenda although they were fighting in a multitude of international markets.

My work with the IFPI lasted only a short while but it did bring me into contact with Sir John Morgan who was appointed as President in around 1990. He had been

Britain's Ambassador to Mexico, Poland and South Korea and also worked for newspaper tycoon Robert Maxwell as Managing Director of Maxwell Communications. We lunched together - just the once - and at the end I came to the conclusion that diplomatic lunches could last even longer than record company lunches – but it was a close call.

During our marathon dining experience Morgan held court with a host of wonderful tales about life as a diplomat but topped them all with his story about being in Budapest with Robert Maxwell. When they met up at around mid-morning, Maxwell announced that he had been out to buy a Hungarian newspaper. When Morgan commented that he didn't know Maxwell spoke Hungarian, the disgraced owner of the *Daily Mirror*, who died in 1991, replied that he didn't and he had purchased an Hungarian publishing business not a morning paper.

In the midst of all this I was still working for the HMV Group and Stuart McAllister (or Lee Scott as he was to me in the 1960s). They had ambitions to expand globally and by the time the company celebrated its 75th anniversary in 1996, there were HMV shops in Australia, Ireland, Canada, SE Asia, Japan and the USA, while stores existed briefly in France, Germany and Italy. I had the delightful task of having to travel around the world, with my wife, to report on all these international operations in order to create a book celebrating HMV's diamond anniversary.

It was a private publication but we managed to get amongst others Duran Duran, Carly Simon, Tina Turner, Sting, Annie Lennox, Phil Collins and former Prime Minister Edward Heath to contribute messages while Gary Barlow reminded us that he had bought his first record – 'Cars' by Gary Numan - in the Chester branch of HMV and Cliff

Richard recalled making a demo disc in the Oxford Street store in 1958 with a group called the Drifters who became The Shadows.

McAllister's attempts to make a major impression with HMV in America were always going to be threatened by the sheer size of the country. Having shops in New York and expanding into Boston, Washington DC, Philadelphia and eventually into the Rock'n'Roll Hall of Fame complex in Cleveland did not make it a nationwide operation to compare with Tower Records, Camelot or Sam Goody, two of which McAllister tried to purchase to boost the HMV brand.

While HMV shops around the world proudly displayed the famous Dog & Trumpet logo, it was not the case in North America and Asia where the trademark was owned originally by the Victor company which later became RCA and ultimately part of Bertelsmann. Here the shops could be called HMV but Nipper and the gramophone were conspicuous by their absence from the stores' signage.

When the first HMV shop was opened in Tokyo in 1990, I helped open the store but only at the back door! Protocol required a local dignitary declare the store (and the main entrance) officially open, while I helped cut the ribbon to the newly created Beatles Room at the rear of the store along with a local Japanese singer and HMV Japan President Chris Walker.

During conversations in Tokyo I discovered that there were no alarms in the store or on the products sold as that would have been considered an insult by the law-abiding Japanese who didn't have a reputation for shoplifting. It was sad to realise that the only thefts from the shop were by Westerners.

During this visit I was invited to give a talk to the Japanese

Beatles fan club who gathered in a theatre to hear me witter on about the abandoned Beatles' *Sessions* album and my *Abbey Road* book. It was a long night as my talk and then both questions and answers had to be translated, but they did present with me a splendid incense burner to mark the occasion.

The arrangements for the event began some weeks before I travelled to Tokyo as the organisers sent over a dummy nameplate with my name in both English and Japanese. They wanted me to confirm that their Japanese spelling of my name was correct. This turned out to be a step too far for a man familiar only with sake (rice wine), gohan (rice), sushi (rice with fish) or tonkatsu (deep fried pork) and, in order to help, I made my way round to the local Japanese restaurant near Baker Street and explained what I needed to know for the people in Japan. It turned out that the Japanese spelling of my name was absolutely correct and the name plate sits in my study to this day - to remind me of who I am in two languages.

Over the years at EMI I had been involved with artists making personal appearances (pas) in HMV stores – Cliff and Kate to name a couple – and the new regime at HMV were keen to carry on with the good work – except they didn't always go to plan. The opening of the HMV store in Herald Square, opposite Macy's in New York, in 1995 was to be performed by the renowned jazz singer Nancy Wilson but the HMV executive was not quite on the ball when he asked her what it was like to have worked with Diana Ross! He thought she was the former Supremes singer Mary Wilson. I don't know who was more surprised, him or her.

Working with HMV in the USA brought me into contact with Rob Goldstone who was retained as their PR consultant in the states. He was an Englishman who later got into some sort of hot water for setting up a meeting between representatives of a Russian billionaire and Donald Trump's son and son-in-law in Trump Tower ahead of the 2016 US Presidential election.

My dealings with Goldstone were much more mundane and my abiding memory is a scenario that played out after we had dinner together in a fancy New York steak house. On the way out, a hobo came up to us and made it clear who he thought I was. Now over the years I have been mistaken for Willie Rushton (harsh), Dr Hook's Dennis Locorrier and Michael McDonald from the Doobie Brothers (both better) and even Bill Oddie (very unkind) but this time it was world-famous country singer Kenny Rogers. He looked at me and said, "Hey Kenny, how ya doin'? Sing me that song 'Lucille', it's my favourite".

I protested my innocence in my finest English accent but he was having none of it and carried on asking (loudly) for me to sing and give him some money. At this point, Goldstone stepped in but he only made things worse by explaining that I WAS Kenny Rogers and I often put on a fake British accent to fool people. Realising that this was not going to get any better, I put a couple of dollars in his cup and we made a swift exit left ... with Goldstone giggling away to himself.

Years later I worked on a music radio programme about the songs of the Bee Gees and got to interview Kenny Rogers during one of his visits to London. We had some mutual acquaintances as he had been signed to EMI America and his manager used to be an executive there, and I decided to tell him the story about me being mistaken for him in the street in New York by a man asking for money (and a song). Rogers was keen to know if I had given him any and when I told him that I had put a couple of dollar bills in the cup, he stared at me and said, "So this feller not only thinks you are me but that I'm a cheapskate as well."

As an ex-personnel/human resources manager, the wellbeing of the staff within HMV was one of Stuart McAllister's main areas of concern and he was keen to motivate and involve them at every turn. He hit on the idea of offering a lucky HMV employee the chance to win a trip to London to see Paul McCartney in concert at Earls Court in 1993. I can't remember what they had to do to win - maybe it was a quiz or essay-writing contest - but while I sorted out the tickets - six in all for McAllister and his wife, me and my wife and the lucky winner plus partner – HMV's boss picked out the winner.

I then came up with the idea of trying to arrange a backstage meet and greet for the winner with McCartney and my only issue, as I explained to the HMV boss, was that the former Beatle was more likely to want to meet a shop floor worker than a board room exec. He was after all a man of the people. Luckily the winner was I think a forklift driver working in the warehouse for HMV Canada. He and his partner were flown over, put in a hotel and given tickets to the show, but the meeting was still hush-hush as we all knew about the best laid plans of mice... But fortunately, things went smoothly and during the interval, McAllister and I escorted the lucky couple through the labyrinth of corridors that is Earls Court into the dressing room area where McCartney - true to his word - was there to do exactly as he had promised.

When McAllister left HMV in 1999, my consultancy came to an end as well but not before he arranged for HMV to support a major dinner in aid of Save The Children. We gathered at the Savoy Hotel in London with Michael Ball as the cabaret turn and the Princess Royal as guest of honour.

Along with McAllister, my wife Pat and I were introduced to her Royal Highness who was keen to know what role I played in HMV. When I told her that I was a consultant, she went further and asked the dreaded question, 'what does that mean?' I explained that it meant that McAllister could call me, ask a question and I would give him an answer which he could take on board or ignore - either way I still got paid. HRH didn't seem overly impressed and even less so when I asked if she had any need of a consultant of her own.

Meeting the Princess completed my royal double whammy as some years earlier I had been in the line-up to meet Prince Charles (now King Charles III) at a BPI event when he came along with Princess Diana. We were split into two groups – one to meet him and one to say hello to her – and briefed by officials on how to behave (give a nod of the head when introduced) and reminded to speak only when spoken to.

With HMV no longer in the picture, my time with WMI, who I joined as the full time Vice President of Communications in 2001, was also coming to an end. The two chairmen (Ramon Lopez and his successor Stephen Shrimpton) who I worked for - both former EMI executives - had retired and it was a new regime with that other ex-EMI colleague Roger Ames at the head of the whole Warner Music Group. Eventually a Frenchman named Albertini took over as head of WMI and we never really saw eye to eye and his style of management - to my mind somewhat distant and egotistical - meant we were never going to get on. Within a year of him becoming my boss, I was shown the door and replaced, as were a number of other Vice Presidents, by a younger, less experienced and cheaper person who was happy with the title Director.

At HMV's gala dinner in aid of Save The Children, HMV chairman Stuart McAllister introduces me and my wife Pat to Princess Anne, the Princess Royal

In order to keep busy I teamed up with my radio producer pal Tony Hale and we set about making a series of music programmes for the digital music radio channel Music Choice Europe. These were one-off specials about artists and labels and I recall spending time with producer Alan Parsons in his home studio, Roxy Music's Phil Manzanera, Darryl Hall (without Oates) and Mickie Most in addition to creating a Motown special.

Capital Gold also employed me to write and help bring together radio specials on Legendary Labels, Elvis Presley and The Beatles although this last one, despite featuring contributions from Glen Matlock, Barbara Dickson, Graham Gouldman and Steve Harley, was never aired. Radio was now taking up quite a bit of time as I also worked on a few programmes for the Wise Buddah production company where I acted as writer and researcher on shows about the Bee Gees and a radio version of the book Northern Songs which was hosted by renowned journalist Paul Sexton. When this was broadcast, on BBC Radio 2 in 2007, reviewer Gillian Reynolds, almost a decade after she questioned the merits of the BBC commissioning my programme about EMI's 90th anniversary, said something nice about this one. "Now here's the story I've been waiting to hear in this network's current sixties season, the one that tells an instructive tale of where the money goes in the pop business." We all hoped she wasn't disappointed.

But, like all good things, the radio programmes eventually came to an end and I was also left without any consultancy work. But I still had pen and paper (actually a computer keyboard and screen) and it was time to become a full-time, part-time author and 20-odd books later we are both at the end of that journey as well.

Looking back over the 50 years that have gone before, there were plenty of highlights but also a few disappointments. Just for the hell of it, I'll finish by listing a few of them.

I was disappointed that...

I'd been unable to appreciate the music of the Carpenters, particularly after going to two shows a night for two weeks.

That Mick Jagger, after four meetings, still didn't remember me from our first get-together backstage at Southend Odeon in 1965.

That 'Mull Of Kintyre' got to No.1 and 'Somebody To Love' didn't.

That all managers weren't like Cliff's Peter Gormley or Floyd's Steve O'Rourke.

That we fell for Malcolm McLaren scams twice, with the Pistols and Bow Wow Wow.

That Kate Bush didn't come back to say hello at the after the show drinks party in 2014.

That both Al Green and Stevie Wonder wanted me to do more singing than them at their last concerts I went to.

That Bob Dylan didn't want to talk to me in a London street and that I had to sit through his concert at the O2 Arena in 2009 when the magic had faded.

That I never got the chance to meet John Lennon, the Beatle I admired most even though I was warned it might not be a warm and cuddly moment.

BIBLIOGRAPHY

Readers of *Bull & Bush* may be interested to check out some of the other books written by Brian Southall:

Abbey Road (Patrick Stephens 1982/Omnibus 1997)
A-Z of Record Labels (Sanctuary Books 2000)
Northern Songs (Omnibus 2006)
Sex Pistols - 90 Days at EMI (Bobcat 2007)
If You Don't Know Me By Now - the Story of Simply Red (Carlton 2007)
Pop Goes To Court (Omnibus 2008)
The Rise & fall of EMI (Omnibus 2009)
Beatles Memorabilia - the Julian Lennon Collection (Goodman 2010)
Treasures of The Bee Gees (Carlton 2011)
Jimi Hendrix Made In England (Clarksdale 2012)
Treasures of Bob Dylan (Carlton 2012)
Dark Side Of The Moon Revealed (Clarksdale 2013)
The Beatles In 100 Objects (Carlton 2013)
From Me To You (Red Planet 2014)
Banned On The Run - the music they wouldn't let you buy (Poppublishing 2014)
The Hollies Story (Red Planet/Poppublishing 2015)
Sgt Pepper's Lonely Hearts Club Band (Carlton 2017)
Dreamboats & Petticoats (Red Planet 2017)
The White Album (Carlton 2018)
The Beatles Album By Album (Carlton 2019)
Bringing On Back The Good Times (This Day In Music 2021)
A Saucerful of Tea (Poppublishing 2022)

Printed in Poland
by Amazon Fulfillment
Poland Sp. z o.o., Wrocław

32945828R00145